The Australian Career Passport

The Australian Career Passport

Cross the career border with your core skills for work

LAWRENCE ARNOLD

Typeset by BookPOD
Typeset in Adobe Text Pro 11/14

Cover design by Aida Viziru

Disclaimer
The material in this book is general comment only and neither purports nor intends to be specific advice related to any particular reader. It does not represent professional advice and should not be relied on as the basis for any decision or action on any matter that it covers. To the maximum extent permitted by law, the author and publisher disclaim all responsibility and liability to any person or entity, whether a purchaser or not, in respect to anything and of the consequences of anything done by any such person in reliance, whether in whole or in part, upon the whole or any part of the contents of this publication.

A Catalogue-in-Publication is available from the National Library of Australia.

ISBN: 978-0-9945003-1-1

Acknowledgements

I believe it's difficult for professionals to 'do' their careers without help from career professionals, and I know it's impossible to publish a career book without help from book professionals!

I'd like to thank a number of book professionals for their help. Carolyn Jackson of Grammar Factory was my decisive and incisive editor. She gave me ideas on structure that challenged me, and inspired me to the decision and incision that have become second nature. Aida Viziru of Pixel Salad Studio produced another fabulous book cover and flyers. Working across the Pacific was like being in the same office in Melbourne again. Sylvie Blair of BookPOD performed her usual magic on my challenging format needs, particularly with the Passport in Chapter 7. Her ongoing generosity, enthusiasm, and practical suggestions always lifted my spirits during bouts of doubt

The final acknowledgement may seem eccentric. It's for Professor Ian Holtham – pianist, teacher, and Bach scholar. In 2017, I attended his new CD launch – a combined lecture, concert, and his usual Monday undergraduate master class. Bach's work comprises two books – as does mine! I paraphrase Professor Holtham in stating that Book 1 drew on an earlier musical tradition to mould a new one, while Book 2 presented Bach's considered position on music and predicted a new world of composition that came to pass with Mozart through to Schoenberg – all of whom used his two books.

During the launch, I realised that my career books are similarly structured. Book 1 reviews the career practices that have evolved over the past, and establishes new methods for personal career development. Book 2 (this one) establishes my position on current career issues, and educates my readers on the recruitment revolution they are now facing.

Contents

Introduction   1

PART 1: KNOW YOUR SKILLS

1   Your employability   9

2   What employers want   17

3   Your core skills   25

4   Cluster One: Navigate the world of work   31

5   Cluster Two: Interact with others   39

6   Cluster Three: Get the work done   49

7   The Australian Career Passport   55

PART 2: SHOW YOUR SKILLS

8   Forensic investigations   79

9   The changing face of job applications   89

10   The most important document ever written   101

11   Jump the job queue   117

12   The 3Rs of recruiting – recruiters, robots, and rorts   129

13   The job interview part 2: Be Prepared   143

14   The job interview part 2: Questions and answers   155

15   Negotiate the numbers   169

     Conclusion   175

     Appendix A: The outcome professionals   179

     Appendix B: Recruitment methods used by professionals   187

     References   189

     But there's more ...   191

INTRODUCTION

This book is your passport to cross the career border, jump the job queue, and arrive at your employment destination with your essential cabin baggage, ready to start your new role. It's about getting a job, or improving the one you have.

Specifically, it's about getting the job you want by knowing, understanding and showing employers your *core* skills. But do you know exactly what they are?

The term core skills may not have the meaning you'd assume. In 2013 the Australian Government coined the term 'Core Skills for Work', by which it meant, not the technical skills required for a particular occupation, but the more subtle interpersonal skills that are the oil that helps an organisation run smoothly. These transferable skills are needed everywhere, and are the sorts of skills that a mature, well-adjusted, well-balanced individual has. They're skills that can be acquired both in your professional life, *and* your personal life. This might surprise you, but employers are emphasising these skills more often in the job selection process, because they indicate a successful person and a successful employee!

If you're not convinced, let me tell you about a BIG4 national Graduate Programs Manager, whom we'll call Vanessa. I met Vanessa at a professional development session for career coaches in Melbourne, where she was presenting on her firm's hiring practices:

> *Vanessa was an experienced management professional and had been the Graduate Programs Manager for several years. She was responsible for the strategic aspect of the recruitment process, with the day-to-day duties handled by her staff of ten. It's an enormous task, placing 550 interns and 550 graduate employees out of 22 000 applicants each year.*

To handle the process, an Applicant Tracking System (ATS) is used, but each application is also personally reviewed, to ensure that candidates are not unfairly rejected.

As a career coach who had often placed clients in these BIG4 programs, I was very keen to garner any information on the selection process. I'd been very successful over several years in placing my clients with the other 'BIG3' but I'd never been able to place anyone with this big one, so I was particularly keen to access any information on their hiring process.

The key information Vanessa gave me was, that as well as assessing the academic qualifications and work background of applicants, she's also interested in 'what kind of people they are'. She wanted to see 'their story' as presented in their resume and supporting statements. She said, 'We want to see if there is something exceptional about the background of the applicants. If they're from a lower economic background, or are the first person in the family to graduate from university, this demonstrates motivation and determination, so we're interested. If they've travelled to remote locations and worked with people in different cultures, we're interested, because we're interested in diversity, in all its forms. We used to just go for finance and accounting grads, but now we're interested in engineers and mathematicians as well'.

I was delighted by this respect for intuition. I'd always counselled my young clients not to overstate their interests, unless they had Olympic medals, and also told them in listing personal activities to emphasise the job-related skills they'd developed from these. With this new information I'll be encouraging my clients to dig deep to explain what they've learnt from playing trumpet in a mariachi band in rural Mexico, and put it on their resume under 'Community and volunteer'.

But there's also a more important point here. The 'person with a story' that employers are interested in is often revealed through their core skills, which cover facets of life such as managing work life, communication, creativity, innovation, and problem solving. In other words, employers will be looking for someone with strong core skills, whether they're explicitly aware of this or not.

So, understanding core skills, knowing what your best ones are and which ones you need to work on, and knowing how to demonstrate them to potential employers is key to exercising some control in the job market. This book tells you how to do this.

The Australian Career Passport

In my first book, *The Australian Career Mentor: career guidance for experienced professionals and new graduates*, I introduced the *Australian Core Skills Audit* based on the *Core Skills for Work Developmental Framework* – an initiative of the Australian Government and the Business Council of Australia. This 'public-private partnership' gave career counsellors the framework to develop specific career programs in a national context – the government builds the roads, so private businesses and citizens can drive on them. I introduced the *Australian Core Skills Audit* to the career profession at the Career Development Association of Australia National Conference in 2016, to give career counsellors a grass roots skills audit based on top-down thinking.

My first book targeted career direction, and this one targets career implementation. The *Audit* also forms the basis of this book, but this time I take the concept further and introduce *The Australian Career Passport*. This instrument helps you define your skills and link them to your job search strategy, thus opening up the world of opportunity others miss out on, and giving you an unfair advantage in the job market.

This book is based on concepts developed in the Australian employment context, with input from Australian career coaches. It's targeted at people already working in Australia, but also helps internationals prepare for local employment. The *Passport* benefits the individual, can be adapted to each person's situation, and can provide aggregated data across the economy – individual, adaptable, and national. The convergence of hiring processes across the world enables *The Australian Career Passport* to be used in all economies that can implement or adapt its content.

Who should use this book?

It's suitable for a wide range of people:

- those finishing a tertiary course, and feel they're going down the wrong path;
- those who've been in the workforce for some time, and have gone down the wrong path;
- mature workers with great steps ahead who need to get back on the path;
- senior school students tackling course selection , and trying to find the path; and
- career coaches, careers teachers, and HR professionals clearing the path.

White collar, blue collar, orange collar, school collar

Depending on your collar colour, you may want to use all of the information in this book, or perhaps be more selective. Senior school students are a special group, and I've directed comments to them in shaded break-out boxes with this logo – ♟.

There's too much pressure on young people, forcing course selection before you know much about the world of work, or much about the courses.

You're becoming more independent all the time, and with a part-time job you're in the adult world, with all its challenges. It's generally a positive experience. Research shows that senior school students with a few hours of part-time work have a slightly higher long-term success rate for study and career outcomes. You know what it's like; the rules you find annoying at home and school are just fine when you're getting paid to follow them.

In this ♟ category I include young people in Registered Training Organisation (RTO) courses or TAFE Institutes. You may feel quite lost in these sprawling environments, and find it difficult to access career help. Institutes and private colleges often don't have the well-resourced career departments of universities.

My quick tip on course selection is: you're selecting a course, not selecting a life. You can always change a course.

I have written extra ♆ descriptors in the *Passport* in Chapter 6. I've also written some special sections you'll find in the grey text boxes like this throughout the book. I've done this because some topics may not apply to your situation, so you can decide what to read, and which exercises to do.

How to use this book

This book is about you, so starts off with your employability, and your skills. There are exercises along the way called skilltasks. They reinforce the text but may generate new ideas. No need to do all of all of them – stop when you've 'got it'. I cover the new Core Skills for Work thoroughly to prepare you for the choices you make in *The Australian Career Passport* in Chapter 6, and that task prepares you for your job search.

After you've completed *The Australian Career Passport*, I'll show you how to use your career insight for action, by changing your resume, your job application approach, your interview, and hopefully – your outcome!

I hope the chapters will be self-explanatory and kickstart your career action with career insight, but in case of difficulty – just call me.

PART 1

KNOW YOUR SKILLS

CHAPTER 1

Your employability

Career keywords: employability; career identity; personal adaptability; human & social capital; career synergy

The language of employers is 'skills', so you need to know your skills, both for your own benefit, and to communicate them to employers. But before you get to that, you need to understand your employability, and see how your skills fit into it. But what is employability?

Employability

At the basic level, your employability is your capacity to find work and keep it. At a deeper level your employability has three facets: career identity; personal adaptability; and human and social capital.

Career identity

Personal
adaptability   →   *EMPLOYABILITY*   ←   Human capital &
Social capital

Let's examine these three facets individually.

Career identity

Everybody has a career identity. Whether you're an established professional networking over a Chivas Regal in the QANTAS Club, or a junior shelf stacker in Safeway Burwood this identity contributes to your employability. Not only can you work in Safeway Burwood, but you can transfer to Safeway Kew where you're closer to your classes and interview locations for that great internship. If your career identity is that of a seasoned professional, you'll be contacted regularly by headhunters wanting to get you in front of employers for a great new job offer. Though there's a huge difference in salary and benefits, both of these different people manifest career identity.

I saw a good example of strong career identity while driving recently in suburban Melbourne.

> I came up to some traffic lights, and saw a large white van in the far lane. It was completely enclosed, so I had no idea of the equipment inside, nor the occupation of the driver. There was a dark blue sign on the side panel – GARRY. It was very large, and stood out at a distance. I immediately knew this was a plumber – not a lawyer, not a dog groomer, nor a landscape gardener. The name conjures up a knock-about, good bloke, able to roll up his sleeves and get down into that blocked drain at the back of the garden – with only moderate overcharging. This image is so strong that it works whether the person is John Garry, Jane Garry, or Garry Wong.

> I was wondering why I'd made this guess when GARRY took a left turn, and I saw 'plumbing' and a mobile number on the back door.

> I think that GARRY understands his career identity, and communicates it clearly. I must have driven beside 100,000 white vans in my life, and I can't remember any of them, except GARRY. When that blocked drain gets really troublesome, I know the name I'll Google, and the colour of the van that will pull into the driveway. Now ... that's career identity!

While I don't have a white van with *LARRY* emblazoned on it, I'm tempted to use myself as a subject to explore career identity. With this second career book, I'm gradually building up my expanded career identity as a career writer. This adds to my present career identity of 'that Melbourne CBD career coach', and differentiates me from most career coaches who've never written a career book. Depending on your career stage, you may want to use your career identity to 'identify more closely to others' rather than 'differentiate from others'. A recent accounting graduate, for example would want to present as more like an experienced accountant, rather than standing out because of inexperience. If an experienced accountant, I'd advise to stand out by highlighting differences.

I may never be as charismatic as *GARRY*, but my career identity can improve with planning – so can yours.

Personal adaptability

A young shelf stacker has considerable personal adaptability. If that great internship comes through then leaving the tins and jars for the big career change can be immediate. For the experienced professional, personal adaptability is somewhat different. You may want to take a great job offer in Singapore, but if you have kids in primary school, and deep personal connections in your local community it may be difficult to hop on the next flight. Taking up the offer is more than a career and business decision – it's a family and social decision. You're less adaptable in this sense. However, with some house equity and some personal savings, you may be able to take the risk of setting up a business to develop the next phase of your career. Any limitations on personal adaptability will limit your employability, and any liberation will increase it.

My employability is limited because I'm limited to the Melbourne metropolitan area. However, my career writing is expanding my personal adaptability, so my employability is developing dynamically – so can yours.

Human capital and social capital

Your human capital is more than just your bank account. It could be your capacity to get a bank loan to start a business, or do an expensive MBA. As a shelf stacker, your state-of-the-art Smartphone, and bank balance of $173.85 are your key physical assets, but your current degree is also an element of your human capital. This gives you a claim to that great internship, opening up fabulous possibilities of a real job on a great package.

A key component of your human capital is your set of skills, and this book will focus on those in later chapters.

Your social capital is more subtle. This is your capacity to 'work the system' using your accumulated experience, your life skills, your 'street smarts', your engaging personal manner, your trustworthiness, and your capacity to network effectively. The extent of the hidden job market is greatly exaggerated in Australia, but it certainly exists, and your social capital is the key to success here. One of my clients, let's call him Roberto, told me a great story of how he got his first professional job in Australia shortly after he'd finished his higher degree in accounting and logistics. This was a case of luck, personality, and social capital.

> *Roberto was waiting at the traffic lights when a funny incident across the road got him talking to the bloke standing beside him. They had a laugh and when they crossed the street, they dropped in for a drink at a bar on the corner. They really hit it off, and this new mate turned out to be a junior manager with a massive national transport and logistics firm.*
>
> *Two weeks later my client had some interviews, and was working with this iconic firm within the month.*
>
> *This is a one-in-a-million chance, but it demonstrates the social capital my client had developed over time. He's a very outgoing person, and is comfortable talking to people around him. People at his new job call him 'the Crazy Colombian' and he knows it's meant in a nice way because they like his high energy, enthusiasm, and drive. His sense of humour takes the steam out of a very stressful role. I explained that in Australia, people sometimes hide their respect for others behind a funny name. It's an undercover knighthood.*

My approach to social capital has to be more systematic because I can't rely on some stranger in the street asking me into a bar.

I attend the large career expos, do conference presentations, write articles, and publish books like this. Other career coaches get to know me, and we often meet up for a networking coffee in the Melbourne CBD. As a Fellow of the Royal Society of Arts, elected for my contribution to career writing, I'm part of an international network of 28 000 people with similar professional values. Each year I get several offers of jobs and career partnerships. I haven't been picked up on a street corner yet, but am growing my social capital in a wide range of professional situations – so can you.

The energy of synergy

You can improve your human capital by taking conscious steps to improve your skills. When you improve your skills, your career identity improves, opening more opportunities to become more adaptable. It's an upward spiral.

As an example of this synergy, while I was doing my career counselling qualification, I also completed the Myers-Briggs Type Indicator accreditation with the Australian Council for Educational Research. While a major investment, it immediately distinguished me from the hundred other people in my career counselling course, expanding my career identity.

I'll admit that I wasn't the best person in that career counselling course. The best person was a high school receptionist. She had a Certificate IV qualification that had enabled her to enroll in the course. She was a bit defensive, and often presented herself as 'going up against the teachers' in applying for career positons in her school.

In the group counselling exercises and role plays, she immediately demonstrated empathy, and identified the career issue. It took me many months to develop this key counselling skill. She was a 'natural'.

However, I more quickly developed my career identity as a career coach, and I suspect this 'natural' ended her career in the school receptionist role. Over her work life she would have helped thousands of kids who were required to 'report to the principal', or who had lost their lunch money, and needed a sympathetic tone and a short-term loan, but I don't know that she ever got a school career counsellor position.

I really admired her career spirit, and wish I had a TARDIS to go back and tell her about the three facets of employability.

Shortly after listing the Myers-Briggs accreditation on my website, I had calls from organisations wanting a Myers-Briggs consultant. I didn't take every offer, but just getting them added to my personal adaptability. This virtuous spiral improved my employability as a Melbourne CBD career counsellor.

So, your career identity, personal adaptability, and your human and social capital define your employability. These integrate synergistically to define your career, and will change over time.

You can coast along in your career life totally oblivious to this, or you can take action to improve your employability by working on these three elements. Now you understand the concept, you can plan for improved employability in your career.

career identity

work: use it or lose it

social capital

synergy

financial resources

employability

core skills   technical skills

personal adaptability

human capital

Skilltask 1 Your employability: The three facets of your employability.

In this exercise we'll deconstruct your employability and then reconstruct it to your new specifications. Think about your career identity as it is presently, and write some keywords in each cell. Then think what you'd really liked to have written, and put down the keywords for those thoughts in the adjacent cell. Do the same for the other two employability facets. This is your vision.

Your employability	What you see now	What you want to see
Your career identity		
Your personal adaptability		
Your human capital & social capital		

Now that you've established your vision you need to implement it. Keep reading.

Your employability is determined by your career identity, your personal adaptability, and your human and social capital. In subsequent chapters we'll see how your skills fit into all of this.

CHAPTER 2

What employers want

Career keywords: The perfect employer?; the employer's perspective; the hiring mantra; KSAOs; skills & aptitudes; values & attitudes; the perfect employee?; the perfect job?

The perfect employer doesn't exist. The perfect employee doesn't exist, and neither does the perfect job. However, for the employment relationship to work effectively there must be some level of attraction, and the higher the attraction, the better the relationship. There's a lot of advice around about how to make yourself attractive to an employer, but the process of landing a great job isn't all one-sided. An employer should also be attractive to you. This should be 'informed attraction' – based on real knowledge. Before you get into employment speed-dating, have a careful think about the type of company you're keeping.

The perfect employer?

Despite imperfections, you should be seeking out those employers having as much fit for you as you have for them. While employers are assessing you, you're assessing them.

Your list of what you're looking for in an employer will be highly personal and may include:

- salary and benefits (generous, of course);

- range of duties;
- travel possibilities;
- the 'mission' of the organisation;
- size of organisation;
- career development opportunities;
- physical location;
- style of work environment, like open plan or hot-desking;
- management style;
- demographics of work colleagues; and
- work/life balance and flexibility.

Some of these will be difficult to assess without knowing an insider, but www.glassdoor.com will give you the views of present employees. The company website will paint a rosy picture, but media articles may show you the thorns.

Larger organisations should have a Human Resources division, and this unit is the meat in the sandwich between the employer's expectations, and yours. The HR unit is clearly on the side of their employer, but you should find people in it open to sharing important information with you. It's also in their interest for both sides to make an informed employment decision.

Once you have a suitable employer picked out, you need to position yourself as a suitable applicant. To do this, you need to start looking at things from the employer's point of view. So let's now consider the hiring process from an employer's perspective by investigating the hiring mantra.

The hiring mantra

When assessing applicants the employer has a hiring mantra etched into the psyche:

- Can the person do the job?
- Will the person do the job?
- Will the person fit in?

If there is any doubt on any of these, you won't get the job on offer – and you shouldn't.

Can do?

In assessing your capacity to do the job, your skills are evaluated both formally and informally. You may undertake psychometric testing, or be put in front of a computer to fill out an Excel spreadsheet, if that's part of the job. Behavioural questions may be asked to assess whether you 'can do'.

Will do?

Assessing that the applicant will actually do the job is harder, and the HR professional may have to use intuition here. This is more than just the person turning up to start at 9.00 am Monday morning in three weeks' time. If the applicant isn't really committed to the job, then a competing offer could be accepted, even after the starting date.

This also covers the commitment to deal with job problems that arise in the natural course of duties over the first few weeks and months: issues with difficult people; coping with imperfect resources and equipment; a job reality different from the perfect picture painted at the interview; and a skills gap where applicants have overestimated their competencies. The employer will have to estimate how well you'll deal with these surprises, and how much you have the real interest in the job to stay, and deliver. This goes to motivation to do the job, and having strategies to deal with problems that arise. If you run away at the first challenge, then the employer is back to square one with an expensive recruiting re-run.

This is where HR professionals really earn their money, by using the judgement gained through experience to recommend applicants who 'will do'.

Will fit?

Predicting that you 'will fit' is problematic, and many employers use sophisticated psychometric assessments for this exercise. I'm not convinced that a particular personality assessment will accurately predict that a particular person will do a particular job, in a particular way, in a particular team, in a particular setting. I think we're still too human for that. Some organisations have policies to mix up their workforce to enhance social inclusiveness, but most are just happy that you 'will fit' and 'will stay'.

You'll see the possibility for error in the hiring mantra, but experienced HR professionals have the human touch to understand a wide range of job applicants. The employer relies on these professionals to facilitate the hiring decision, and reduce risk by implementing effective hiring processes – effective, but not perfect.

The perfect employee?

The perfect employee is as rare as the perfect politician! At elections, the political parties often discover that one of their new stars has a police record, was in some extremist group, has some appalling statement on the internet, or is the owner of 'Hot Peppers Gin Palace'. It's enough to lose the seat, so the offender is quietly side-lined, and the promotional billboards removed overnight. As a job applicant, you may not be so closely monitored, but your work, study, character, and social media record are up for review by employers and recruiters. Recruitment is complex, but the positives that recruiting professionals are looking for in applicants can be boiled down to a simple acronym.

KSAOs – not so secret!

While KSAOs sounds like a secret international criminal organisation dogged by bad spelling and justifiably exploded by 007 in the final ten minutes, it's really just an acronym for the knowledge, skills, aptitudes, and other attributes employers are seeking.

Knowledge

Much occupational knowledge is gained through formal qualifications offered by universities, TAFE Institutes, Registered Training Organisations, and professional development courses and sessions available face to face or online. If you Google 'fidgetwalling qualifications' you'll be presented with a bewildering array of public and private providers offering you an education in different ways, and at different costs. Possessing this type of knowledge is a given – it's what you and your classmates get from the course. But it's not the only type of knowledge.

Another type of knowledge is 'street smarts'. You may have a glitzy MBA with an organisational development subject included, but the employer just about to embark on a major organisational restructure may prefer someone who has had the experience several times, over an untested novice. It's hard to evaluate this 'how to' knowledge, which is based on experience and the judgement that has resulted, but an employer will thoroughly investigate experience every time.

> You may be doing some adult courses while you're still attending school, or in your present casual job. One of the big fast food chains, Mmmm ... wonder who they are, offers Certificate II and Certificate III courses to young staff members. These courses are highly regarded by other employers, and you should do them. You'll be seen as someone who can take initiative, and follow through. Completing an adult course is a sign of maturity – even for adults!
>
> Check with the provider to see that they don't record you for the government course subsidy. If you later wanted to do another Certificate III you'd have to pay the full course fee. It wouldn't be fair that you lose the later government subsidy because you did a course your employer wanted you to do when a school student.

Skills

Skills operationalise knowledge. Anyone can gain the knowledge to build a sailing boat by reading a book on the subject, but few will buy the different types of timber to assemble it, hit the water – and stay afloat. Doing that requires skills that won't just manifest through some sort of osmosis while you're reading the book. We'll explore skills and competencies more fully in further chapters, to ensure your knowledge is broad and deep enough to keep you afloat.

Aptitudes

Aptitudes are your abilities to function well in your present situation, but also in future situations. This is your underlying conceptual understanding of processes or equipment encountered in your workplace. Mechanical aptitude, for example, is proficiency with your present equipment, and any new equipment coming along in the future. There are tests to assess your various aptitudes that typically put you in a new situation to see how you cope.

Others

These are the particular attributes that individual employers are seeking in particular roles, and are usually described as values and attitudes.

Values

Values are very personal things, and you may be wondering why something so personal is important in the business world. But in fact your values can be a big influence on your ability to do a job well, work well with others, and fit into an organisation.

We can't always avoid conflict in work situations, but the more we know our values and those of our colleagues, the more our workplace diversity can move towards harmony.

It's the tradition in career books to have a large stack of qualitative statements to choose from to confirm personal values. While values are a key element of 'others', I won't discuss them extensively here because I've covered them thoroughly in an 'other' book – *The Australian Career Mentor: career guidance for experienced professionals and new graduates.* Chapter 4, *Your career values* has a full explanation.

Attitudes

Your attitudes are your external behaviours – they appear in co-existence with other people – whereas values are internal thoughts and reflections. You can't have attitudes alone in a locked room (unless you're on the phone) because they have a behavioural component. In other words, it's your personality in action. Employers may not have this theoretical framework but they can identify an attitude when they see it – particularly a bad one!

I cover attitudes extensively in *The Australian Career Mentor*, Chapter 5, *What's the attitude?*

Knowledge, skills, and aptitudes are really 'the past, the present, and the future'. Knowledge has been built up by past education and experience, skills are competencies that can be deployed now, and aptitudes indicate your capacity to grow in the future, providing even better service to employers. It's not surprising that the hiring process is so concerned with KSAOs.

The perfect job?

The perfect job doesn't exist either, but you should feel great about getting in for another positive day's work. With the complexity of the Australian economy, and the amount of education available to support career change, there's no reason to stay in a job you dislike.

Most career coaches try to find out more about your personality by using accredited career assessments, a skills audit like *The Australian Career Passport*, discussion and reflection, and helping you to target realistic sectors for employment. The discovery of elements of your personality is a key exercise, but a new approach reverses this process, to focus on the 'personality type' of the job, instead of the personality of the person!

A new 2016 study, *The New Work Mindset* report by the Foundation for Young Australians (FYA) analysed 2.7 million Australian job ads to determine the skills required by employers, and arranged them into seven groups:

The Generators – these jobs require a high level of interpersonal interaction in retail, sales, hospitality, and entertainment.

The Artisans – these jobs require skills in manual tasks related to construction, production, maintenance, and technical services.

The Carers – these jobs require skills in improving the mental and physical well-being of others, including medical care and personal support.

The Coordinators – these jobs require the capacity to undertake repetitive administrative tasks and behind-the-scenes processes, or service tasks.

The Designers – these jobs require deploying skills and knowledge of science, mathematics, and design to construct or engineer products or buildings.

The Informers – these jobs require professionals with skills in providing information, education, or business services.

The Technologists – these jobs require skilled understanding and manipulation of digital technology.

While these skill groups have been humanised to look like types of people, they are descriptions of the skills demanded by employers in online job ads.

The report's identification of seven skills groups helps job applicants understand the groups of skills employers are looking for. It encourages people to reflect on the seven groups, and then align their skills and interests to those categories. This is a good start, but needs a considered assessment like the *Passport* to identify skills reliably. The *Passport* is the missing link, and that's why this book was written.

If we can link the skills employers want with the skills you can identify, you'll have a powerful tool that you can use for your job applications.

In the next chapters, we'll discover your skills and then link them to the needs employers specify.

This chapter has brought order to KSAOs to help you present yourself better to employers. In the next chapter, we'll examine your skills, the most important letter in the acronym, in more detail.

CHAPTER 3

Your core skills

Career keywords: types of skills; skills assessments; the 10 Core Skills for Work; core skills clusters

The language of employers is 'skills', so you need to know your skills, both for your own benefit, and to communicate them to employers in your job search. Job descriptions and job ads list a set of general and specific skills essential to the sector, or the employer in that sector. Even if you've gotten to talk to the employer via the 'hidden job market' and are pitching before the job ad has been written, the decision maker is still investigating your KSAOs to evaluate your employability.

There are different types of skills, with different words often describing the same types of skills – workplace skills, competencies, hard skills, soft skills, key skills, essential skills, transferable skills, technical skills, and now, core skills. None of these terms is used consistently by employers, HR professionals, recruiters, or even career coaches. The Australian Government has aided clarity in developing the Core Skills for Work and, in this chapter, we'll start to analyse them. In later chapters, we'll get you working on them, and them working for you. It's important to understand these skills, because they will be the secret weapons for your job search missions.

Types of work skills

First, let's clarify the difference between 'skills' and 'competencies'. Skills are what you have in the locker, and competencies are 'skills in action'. Maybe you had trumpet lessons when young and made it into the school band. So, someone thought you had high competency in playing. When you left school, life took over, and you dropped the trumpet. This was, unfortunately, into a swimming pool during your graduation party, and the valves never were the same. You still have the skill, but you've lost the competency. You may come back to it one day, get a new instrument, revive your competency, and get the band back together.

Your job and your career are dependent on two types of work skills – technical skills and core skills. Technical skills are often called 'hard skills'. Technical skills in different occupations include:

- Carpenter – cutting a straight line
- Surgeon – cutting a curved line
- Mechanic – clearing the fuel line
- Tennis coach – sending it down the line
- Teacher – drawing a behavioural line
- Train driver – seeing what's on the line
- Fishing boat captain – hauling in the line
- Politician – spinning the party line

Technical skills are developed through formal courses, professional development sessions, on-the-job training, informal feedback from others, and organised mentoring. Others have done that for you; my role is different. I'm going to focus on the skills many job applicants neglect, but which are the future of their employability – core skills.

The full term, 'Core Skills for Work' is too long for any book, so I'm just going to call them 'core skills'. This is the new Australian term for 'employability skills', or the colloquial 'soft skills'. Technical skills and core skills have led you to your current job, and how you develop these two sets of skills will lead you into other jobs, and so develop your career.

Core skills

Core skills are the interpersonal skills you use with others every day to get your job done. While these are often seen as less important than technical skills, they are the oil that helps an organisation run smoothly. An IT executive for a national company once told me that when IT projects fail it's not because of poor technical skills, but because of poor core skills – poor communication, poor negotiation, poor documentation, and poor management of client expectations.

Employers take core skills very seriously and are basing their job requirements on them. I see this trend in online job ads every day.

Understanding your core skills helps you know yourself better, and present yourself better to employers – to future-proof your career.

Here are the Core Skills for Work, as defined by the Australian Government.

Core skill	Plain English meaning
1 – Manage career and work life	Gain work, develop skills, juggle time to do some courses, manage career and life overlap ...
2 – Work with roles, rights and protocols	Understand work regulations and roles, management needs, company documentation ...
3 – Communicate for work	Listen, understand and speak in the 'culture' of the organisation ...
4 – Connect and work with others	Understand strengths and weaknesses, work flexibly with others, build rapport with staff and clients ...
5 – Recognise and utilise diverse perspectives	Understand manager pressures, deal with conflict, cultural and language issues, negotiate ...
6 – Plan and organise	Organise workload, prioritise tasks, work documentation, negotiate timelines ...
7 – Make decisions	Understand decision-making scope, review progress, report difficulties ...
8 – Identify and solve problems	Identify problems and solutions, review outcomes ...
9 – Create and innovate	Seek out opportunities, develop/apply new ideas, keep up-to-date ...
10 – Work in a digital world	Use technologies and systems, connect with others in different ways, access, organise and present information ...

Looking at the ten core skills, you can immediately see some that apply to you, but others may seem mysterious. Write down the ones you think you have:

Ben is in year 11 and has a part-time job that's a bit unusual. He plays Rozzer in the TV series Nextdoor. *He's had this role since he was 12, and they've kept him on, but there was some doubt about it after the skateboard accident. He was in a coma until Christmas – just in the show! His best mate is Grit (actually Graham) and they get into a bit of trouble, but Grit starts it. The studio shoots the episodes every Sunday because they use a real street and a real vet's surgery, and a doctor's. The street's even become famous, and tourist buses turn up during the shoot.*

The job's fun, but there are lines to learn, and he gets them two weeks before and learns them on the train after school. But, it's not just the words, it's how you say them, and there's a coach who helps. But it's really Ben who decides Rozzer's attitudes, and changes how he does the lines. He can't change the words, but he can change the emotion. Because he's the youngest, he gets on well with everybody in the cast, and Sasha Stardust really likes him – she plays Dr Strickland. The papers write total lies about her. She's not like that. She showed him a lot when he started and didn't know what to do. She helped him get lunch on the first day, and it started from then – it was chicken nuggets and chips, with optional green salsa.

Ben doesn't do drama at school, as he's really interested in animals and how they operate. It's not really the anatomical stuff, like a vet, but why they do things. Kids are always going on about climate change, but he's interested in how the animals interact with each other in their physical environment. He has a more hands-on approach, like Steve Irwin. Ben saw him once at the crocodile farm – he could relate to the crocs, and talked well with the audience. He was really good. Ben got his autograph and it's on his desk at home – even now.

He's got a girlfriend (not in the show!). They're just friends – it's not some big romance. She's just in Year 10, but she's the tallest in her class, even in the school. She'll be in Year 11 next year. She's netball captain ... and class captain ... and on the Student Council. She's so neat with all her good girl badges lined up on her collar. The whole family's like that. When Ben visited, her mum did the vacuuming outside her room for the whole time! She wants to be a forensic scientist. Ben says she's definitely got the interpersonal skills for that, and she laughs. She laughs at all his stuff, particularly about Sasha. She and her mum visited the set once. You can arrange it. Her mum really liked Doug Drucker, who plays the vicar (the cast call him 'Black Douglas' behind his back!). The family is pretty religious and they spend the whole Sunday there – God knows what they do all day. The only fly in the ointment is their crazy dog, but it's easy – you just put her lead on in the house, get her to come around, and then she'll sit on command. To teach a dog, you have to get it to spend some energy first, and then it's ready for instruction because it's their nature to follow the leader. Ben read some books on this, and talks to the vet when he takes the pets up. He's even able to tell the vet stuff.

They don't see each other so much, because of church and the series, and they can't spend time together at school until Year 11, but she calls him every Sunday night. She never misses, even when they weren't seeing each other during exams. She's really quite worked up then, not Little Ms Cool any more. Ben thinks she needs to talk with him or she just won't sleep. Talking seems to calm her down. So it's a bit difficult, but they've got the same friends. Anyway – it's not some big romance.

Look at the ten core skills again, and write down the ones you think apply to Ben, and this time say what evidence there is to show this.

Core skills clusters

These ten core skills look challenging – just like the Ten Commandments. There are some you're really good at, some you just manage with, and a couple that cause real problems for you, *and* the people around you!

There are so many categories that seem to overlap, so many new words being used in particular ways, and how you relate the core skills framework to your job may not be totally clear at this point. To bring order, we'll group the ten core skills into three clusters:

- cluster 1 – navigate the world of work;
- cluster 2 – interact with others; and
- cluster 3 – get the work done.

You could see these three clusters like a pirate movie: use the secret map to get to the island; slip the guards the rum keg; then dig up the treasure; and row like mad. Integrated activities with a desirable outcome!

Some of these core skills will come naturally to you, and come together naturally for you, but others require awareness and effort. In getting the jobs you want, understanding and presenting your core skills to potential employers will give you a strong claim to the positions you want. But this is more than putting on a show in an interview. It's about finding out who you are.

It's not the aim to make you perfect, but to give you a realistic idea of your strengths so you can make better career choices.

The next three chapters will examine the skills in each cluster so you understand all of the core skills clearly. Then you'll decide which ones are your property, and which you are yet to acquire.

There's a lot to core skills, and it could be hard work understanding and using them. I've simplified the process for you over the next few chapters, where we deepen your understanding of core skills and how they work out in the workplace.

CHAPTER 4

Cluster One: Navigate the world of work

Career keywords: career navigation; professional development; rights & responsibilities

Cluster one looks like fun – with a bit of danger from those big waves we can't control. The world of work and the tide of recruiting are changing dramatically, and understanding your core skills will give you a strong tiller for the tsunami. You can't control world weather, but you can control your response to it.

Navigate the world of work consists of:

- manage career and work life; and
- work with roles, rights, and protocols.

Manage career and work life

This means you know how to:

- gain work in your occupation or sector;
- implement realistic career planning;
- write your resume and job applications, or source help to do it;
- engage in appropriate networking;

- seek out relevant courses, and juggle time to complete courses successfully;
- keep your fitness and energy up through sport and exercise; and
- manage your personal life so it doesn't interfere with your work performance.

Why would an employer be interested in this core skill? Isn't it a bit personal to be interested in how people run their lives? Does an employer have the right to ask? When an employer asks about managing your career and work life, the real question is, 'Have you gotten your life together, or are your personal circumstances going to inundate your work performance?' That's a fair question.

All employers have this concern. It's particularly important with unusually stressful roles – night work, interstate travel, fly-in/fly-out jobs, or police and emergency services roles. While these roles seem adventurous and stimulating from the outside, many job applicants don't think about the stresses on their relationships and family, much less about being shot at on night shift. If you're attracted to these types of jobs then you need strategies to keep your life together, and so does your family. These strategies are one aspect of managing your career and work life to keep yourself the employable, well-rounded person your colleagues and clients want to associate with.

Work with roles, rights and protocols

This is the extent to which you understand your work environment and the legal responsibilities of the people on site and within the organisation. You can understand this at the obvious level of a 'No Smoking' sign within the building. The company HR manual or website will give fuller operational guidance. At the higher level, understanding the legal and operational requirements of each work role you encounter in the workplace is an essential part of your job.

Work with roles

You have to understand where you and your job are located in the system of your organisation, and work within legal and operational expectations of those around you.

Your written job description should be a comprehensive list of expectations that can be assessed formally by your manager in regular performance reviews. It's probably open to some interpretation, and you should discuss this with your manager. There may be a final dot point – 'other duties from time to time required'. This doesn't mean that you can be given a ladder and told to clean out the guttering, but means other tasks within your level of qualifications and competence may be allocated or negotiated when your manager requires.

Once you're on top of your job, you may gradually extend your tasks to build the evidence needed for promotion. Do this in coordination with your direct manager, who has the option to find more work for you at your level. Once alerted to your enthusiasm and efficiency, the manager may find new tasks and responsibilities for you, but should also ensure you have the skills development needed to undertake the extra duties competently, and the personal supervision to ensure this new extension is successful. I once reported directly to a CEO who announced to staff meetings that anyone could ask to be involved in high-level projects that came across her desk, and take appropriate responsibility for the outcomes. This extended the competencies of staff, *and* cleared the desk.

Working outside of your job description may carry some risks:

> *I recall an energetic and likeable young Premier of the State of Victoria who moved outside his job description with enduring results.*

> *He took a strong dislike to one design aspect of the new city space – Federation Square. As well as a new art gallery and public performance area with a massive video screen for the nation's sporting victories, various essential buildings throughout the square were to be constructed as 'glass shards'. These would reflect images of the iconic railway station, the old cathedral, and the floating metal tu-tu of the concert hall in the*

distance – all actionised by the rhythm of our rumbling tram fleet. You wouldn't see the glass, but the life of the city reflected in it.

The Premier quashed this innovation. He replaced this artistic vision with zinc and tin Australian shed architecture, turning an exciting vision into a tacky public space. Politicians should stick to their job description of messing up politics, and leave architecture to the professionals.

You should also work to understand the roles of other staff, both colleagues and managers. Even if you're in a fairly humble position, ensure you know the name of your CEO and know what organisational initiatives are current priorities. You never know who'll be sharing your lift.

Rights and responsibilities

These are two sides of the same coin. You have responsibilities towards others, which are their rights, and they have responsibilities towards you, which are your rights.

You may be allocated company property like keys, mobile phones, a credit card, and even a car. You should ask about the rules controlling these, and be pedantic about working within them. As I'm writing this, there's a media controversy concerning a senator who has asked a company with links to the Chinese Government to pay a $1670 personal bill. He's being slammed for 'walking like a Peking duck, talking like a Peking duck, and being a Peking duck'. He's certainly been a goose. It's also a responsibility to use company systems properly. Hillary Clinton had the responsibility to use the US Government server for emails, and ducking this responsibility gave people a justification to vote against her in the 2016 US presidential election.

People often get into trouble using their company credit card, or other company property. I once consulted for a large community organisation in Melbourne that encountered an unusual car issue with a middle manager we'll call Dave:

Dave had come from the US, and was an effective and very popular middle manager, co-ordinating community programs from the Melbourne head office. He'd been allocated a company car – a small four-cylinder number with the organisation logo on the doors.

After a successful year, Dave had taken his annual leave, with the plan of seeing something of Australia – and he certainly did that. A month later, his dusty car appeared in the car park with many thousands of extra kilometres on the clock from his road trip to Kakadu. He had lots of stories and great photos of the little vehicle in remote locations. Senior management was shocked at the travels of their asset and grilled Dave on his exploits. He was similarly shocked at their shock, because in the US it's the norm for managers to have unlimited car use. He also pointed out that there was no written protocol covering car use, and that nobody had ever mentioned any limitations on the benefit to him. Everyone was quite upset – particularly the maintenance staff doing the car wash!

Dave was quite right technically, but he endured an uncomfortable couple of days of quiet annoyance, rather than the adulation he'd expected for having seen more of the country than most other people in the office.

Dave thought he had a right, but others thought he had a responsibility. If in doubt – check.

You could also be criticised for an irresponsible attitude. I recall a workplace arbitration case in which a truck driver, whom we'll call Ron, contested his dismissal as unfair:

Ron had been called to attend a workplace disciplinary conference with his manager and HR personnel. He attended as required, but was summarily dismissed during this conference – for 'smirking'.

In the formal arbitration hearing, Ron's lawyer stated that his client had carried out his legal responsibility to attend the disciplinary conference, but was not obliged by law to enjoy it. I hope the lawyer had some fun questioning the HR manager: 'Can you show the tribunal what a 'smirk' is? 'Is it a combination of 'smug' and 'irksome'? Is there a company policy on 'smirking' in the workplace, and has there been adequate professional development on it?'

The arbitration tribunal held that Ron had carried out his responsibility, and so, had been unfairly dismissed. I suspect that Ron would have sat in the tribunal chamber with a particularly large and offensive smirk!

Perhaps the company should install 'NO SMIRKING' signs in their interview rooms. Whatever we may think of Ron's attitude, he had fulfilled his responsibilities, and had insisted on his rights.

Protocols

Originally a diplomatic word meaning 'official formulas', we understand these as the rules, procedures or common practices of an occupation or workplace. These could be as written codes, or cultural expectations – both are equally valid. For example, for over 100 years, there was no formulation of what school teachers were supposed to do, though millions across the globe did it! The expectations ranged from writing neatly on blackboards, to the higher one of maintaining the fabric of society by stamping out smoking, alcohol, graffiti, adolescent sexual interest, and the word 'ain't' – with little success. Though unwritten, these expectations were just as strong as a legislated code.

In practical terms, we could see protocols as the cluster of rights and responsibilities that employers and employees understand and share.

workplace culture

extra duties   family emergency   location

your finances   company mission

manage career and work life

obligations   your job description

your PD

unwritten rules

who's your manager's boss?

work roles   health

your rights   who's your boss?

Skilltask 2: Got it?

Let's find some evidence that you have these two core skills. The convincing evidence column shows the kind of information indicating you have the specific core skill. The final column lets you look at your career and work life to find similar evidence. Think specifically about small incidents and achievements demonstrating that core skill.

Core skill	Convincing evidence	Your evidence
Manage career & work life	Your record of full-time & part-time courses	
	Your professional development courses	
	Moving location to maintain your work record	
	Changing jobs & work roles to implement your career plan	
Work with roles, rights & protocols	Performance reviews showing your understanding of working with others	
	Investigating solutions to management problems	
	Taking part in workplace working groups or committees to improve group performance	
	Extending your work role by taking on extra tasks like staff mentoring	
	Responsible use of your travel allowance	

If you find evidence that you have a specific core skill ... what can you do to keep it developing?

If you find little evidence that you've got it ... what can you do to get it?

When the core skills work together in an integrated way it's like a jig-saw puzzle with ten pieces – fit them together and the real picture is clear. In the next chapter we'll examine the skills you use to interact with others.

CHAPTER 5

Cluster Two: Interact with others

Career keywords: communicate; connect & respect

Some of these ten core skills now may be looking clearer, and you may recognise their appearance throughout your work day. You'll be quite at home in this chapter, as you'll be thinking about all the human interactions you have with people every day.

Cluster two, interact with others, involves:

- communicate for work;
- connect and work with others; and
- recognise and utilise diverse perspectives.

You may be thinking there's some overlap with these three core skills – and you're right. The ten core skills work best when they're in operation synergistically. People are integrated beings, not Daleks. We don't 'communicate for work' for ten minutes, then allocate a couple of minutes to 'recognise and utilise diverse perspectives', destroy planet Zog, and then 'connect and work with others' until morning tea. We do what we do 'naturally' and it may all come together in a seamless ballet of workplace harmony and integration – or not! The reality is that you'll be good at some core skills, just OK at others, and really poor at a couple of them. You'll find this out when you do *The Australian Career Passport* exercise in Chapter 7. You'll then have to decide what to do about this imbalance. Whatever you decide, you'll be using your communication skills to implement the decision, so let's discuss that core skill now.

Communicate for work

Of the ten core skills, 'communicate for work' is the one we all need to improve. Despite that, every resume I've ever reviewed has listed 'high-level communication skills' proudly in the skills summary. After forty years in the workplace, let me assure you that this is not accurate for every person on every occasion. High intelligence doesn't always help, either. I've seen some of the smartest people on the planet make some awful public communication gaffs. In every election campaign, you'll see someone you admire look totally silly, heartless, sexist, or dismissive, and come out the next day with an apology for the hurt caused. In the early days of Linkedin, I made a few unintentional gaffs that I cringe at now. I recall commenting on the photograph of a young UK woman in a scanty beach dress seeking a professional role in Australia. To lessen the tone of criticism, I tried humour, and that was worse. The response from the young woman and others was blistering. I was quite right to alert someone to the professional standards of a country she wanted to work in, but my comment had cut me off from the people I wanted to help. It took me some time to use every Linkedin post precisely and productively. I still try humour, but it's calibrated to draw people to my comments, not push them away.

Verbal communication

How many serious workplace accidents or injustices could have been prevented if someone had spoken up? It's a big decision to confront the system and draw the annoyance of the people you like, so you shouldn't take it lightly. The system will not always reward you.

Fortunately, we don't face big ethical decisions every day, but poor communication can hurt your work, and the work of others.

Often, it's a matter of different priorities for different people in the same work space. Try to understand the priorities of others. Here's an example of conflicting priorities:

I once worked as a consultant to a home nursing organisation. As part of my orientation program to this new area, I spent a day shadowing a liaison nurse in a large public hospital. I'd last been in hospital when I was four, so didn't know what to expect.

The role of the liaison nurse was to arrange home nursing services for patients being discharged after operations or treatment. The assessment discussion with the patient and family could take 30 minutes, and the nurse also needed a discharge notice from the treating physician.

I observed one patient-handover process. After the patient service assessment, the nurse needed the discharge certificate signed by the doctor. The form was to be filled out by the hospital duty nurse who would then organise the doctor's signature. The duty nurse we saw was just finishing her shift, and was busy admitting new patients to the ward after their surgery. She promised to chase up the appropriate doctor. The nurse I was shadowing gave her the new form for completion ... and a pen for the doctor to use.

We returned to the ward three hours later for the discharge notice. It couldn't be found by the new duty nurse, so we went down to patient records in the basement to check the patient file. We opened the file, and there was the uncompleted discharge form ... and the pen!

So here were two good health professionals with different priorities. The home nursing priority was documentation to start home visits. The urgent priority of the duty nurse was admitting new patients in from surgery, and not the tomorrow needs of someone leaving. When verbal communication fails, it's rarely about malice or misunderstanding, but about different priorities.

You also have to learn how to speak in the culture of your organisation, and understand the unspoken messages. A good example is Stein's classic Doctor/Nurse Game exposition and analysis. In the following example, the medical resident on hospital call is woken at 1.00 am by a ward nurse with a patient unable to sleep:

Dr Jones, this is Jenny Smith on 2W. Mrs Brown, who learnt today of her father's death, is unable to fall asleep.

What sleeping medication has been helpful to Mrs Brown in the past?

Pentobarbital mg 100 was quite effective the night before last.

Pentobarbital mg 100 before bedtime as needed for sleep, got it?

Yes I have, and thank you very much doctor.

In this interchange, the doctor, who doesn't want to have to walk the cold corridors in a dressing gown to attend in person, asks for a hidden recommendation from the nurse for a solution for a patient he doesn't know. The nurse, who does know the patient, makes the disguised recommendation, which the doctor can then own. It's a win all round. The patient gets to sleep, so does the doctor, and the nurse gets back to the paperwork in a quiet ward. These subtle professional interchanges are part of the culture of all organisations. You will have had similar discussions in your work context.

The context of the job is important, and you may have to extend your usual communication range by improving your writing and speaking in an environment demanding highly specific skills.

Written communication

Organisational documentation, with its manuals, check sheets, tick lists, regular stats, and notifications to staff and management can be both daunting, and boring.

In some roles, the organisational documentation may be a matter of life and death! On a hospital ward, the nursing staff record patient vital signs like temperature and pulse regularly throughout the day and night. However, if there's a lot of patient movement in and out of the ward, particular attention needed for one person, or a dramatic emergency, staff may be diverted from this basic task, and some patients may not get the usual check. The nurse may repeat the numbers entered by the previous nurse some hours before, resulting in a pattern of misinformation. Before you cast the first stone, think of all the guesstimates you've made at 4.55 pm over the years! If a system has an option for human error, then human error will occur. If you notice these anomalies in the system, you'll have to decide what to do. This will involve deploying other core skills like 'work with roles, rights, and protocols', and 'connect and work with others'.

Connect and work with others

Understanding the roles of other staff members enables you to work more effectively with them. Without this skill, some tasks may be left undone – or done twice. Be pro-active in making these links. When people do this regularly, it's the sign of a healthy organisation, and when it doesn't occur, an unhealthy one. Here's a real example of senior staff in crucial state organisations who failed to 'connect and work with others' on a day of crisis.

In February 2009, professional and volunteer firefighters outside Melbourne battled the largest bushfires seen for 70 years. Over 200 people lost their lives. The worst day became known as 'Black Saturday' when a massive fire destroyed a picturesque mountain town, killing many people who hadn't been warned.

On that day, the two senior functionaries for public safety – the Police Commissioner and the Country Fire Authority Commissioner – were in their city offices during the conflagration. They later had to account for their actions before a government enquiry.

The Police Commissioner told the enquiry that while not rostered on duty that day, she'd been in her office catching up on paperwork. She also had a meeting with her biographer in the afternoon, and popped out briefly for an appointment with her hairdresser, discussing the terrible events with the stylist in question. She later had an 'inexpensive' dinner out with friends, and watched the news at home before an early night. At the other end of town, the Fire Commissioner was similarly bogged down in paperwork. The key event resulting in most deaths was a sudden wind change in the afternoon that propelled the fire storm towards the unsuspecting town. This sudden change was predicted by the four fire direction experts who had been analysing wind direction throughout the day.

The Fire Commissioner told the enquiry he didn't seek this information, because he assumed, it being Saturday, that the fire direction team wouldn't even have been in the building. Also, he had no operational role in fighting this fire. While the two disaster control commissars were technically correct in their evidence to the enquiry, the community was shocked. It would be like Admiral Nelson and the Duke of Wellington saying that although they knew Napoleon's forces were in their areas, they couldn't deal with them because it was sabre-polishing day.

Had the two commissioners shared a car to the fire zone to direct evacuation traffic, they would have been celebrated as role models able to 'connect and work with others', and 'work with roles, rights and protocols'.

A challenging day for you may not be as dramatic as the above example, but being alert in your workplace will improve the outcomes for all.

Recognise and utilise diverse perspectives

This would be one of the more challenging core skills to develop. As well as being a competent professional, it looks as though you have to become a multicultural consultant! This is where a solid professional development program is needed, and that's a management responsibility. It's not only about multicultural perspectives, but gender issues, age issues, education issues, and ability issues.

I once worked as a consultant to an organisation which interviewed several candidates for a new research officer position. The final choice by the Executive Director was a young man we'll call Richard:

Richard had a serious vision disability and used a white cane to get about. He was quite assertive personally, and had arranged several appointments with the Vice-Chancellor of his university to point out the institution's ineffective protocols on disability issues.

The Executive Director told the staff that, while he'd been impressed by Richard in the interview, and that 'we'll all be working for him in a few years', he had to be convinced that Richard could actually do the job.

The ED did the right thing and called in workplace assessment consultants from Vision Australia to assess both the workplace and the work tasks for suitability. Their assessment was that, with a few minor changes, Richard would be able to operate safely and productively in the role. For the extensive amount of reading needed for the role, Richard was bringing his own software that converted written documents into speech, and voice into writing.

We were all convinced that Richard would be successful in the role, and he was. At the end of his contract he took up a graduate trainee position with the state public service and moved on to a stellar career in public administration.

This is a good example of how the organisation and the individuals in it were able to recognise and utilise diverse perspectives – for the benefit of all.

These issues are also found in a school environment. There are plenty of language and cultural issues, as well as physical and mental health issues. You may have to think about these, and take a stand on some things. Before you take any action, talk about it with your parents – you'll be surprised at how much knowledge they've picked up since you last chatted.

There was a disability issue that hit the media some years ago when a primary school girl who'd been denied access to her senior school because of her physical disability took the school to court. She'd successfully completed six years at her Sydney private school where she'd been an academically excellent and socially popular pupil, and was looking forward to moving on to the senior school with all her friends.

Her parents got a letter over the holidays stating that it would be inappropriate for their daughter to attend the senior campus, so she was not being offered a place. The parents protested but the school wouldn't budge – so the girl launched an action with the Equal Opportunity Tribunal. The tribunal found that the small physical changes at the school and some timetable alterations were 'reasonable', and so the pupil could not be denied access. In the end, it wasn't really that hard. There was a cheer across the nation at the result, and the girl took her rightful place in class.

Were I a principal, I'd like to have students so interested in attending my school that they'd sue me to get in!

This core skill is also about operational issues that arise when different occupations are working together in tight circumstances, and have to cooperate. There's a traditional rivalry between plumbers, chippies and sparkies on a building site, and between police and fire personnel on a disaster site. The emergency services have worked hard to improve this.

These core skills operate in specific workplace contexts, which could be small-scale, large-scale or international. Recently the Northern Territory Government sold the Port of Darwin to a Chinese company, and the alarm bells went off in Washington. The US is presently engaged in a serious diplomatic dispute with China, which claims most of the South China Sea – not so far from the Port of Darwin. While it's a local political decision for a state government to privatise public assets, the US Government expected an ally to give it the 'heads up' on an international security issue alteration. This is a good example of an international failure to 'communicate for work', 'connect and work with others', and 'recognise and utilise diverse perspectives'.

language & culture   what's fair?

disclose disability?   flexible rules

diverse perspectives

Government legislation   quotas & targets

equal opportunity   equality or equity?

who decides?   different approaches

Skilltask 3: Got it?

Let's find some evidence that you have this cluster of core skills. The convincing evidence column shows the kind of information indicating you have the specific core skill. The final column lets you look at your career and work life to find similar evidence.

Core skill	Convincing evidence	Your evidence
Communicate for work	Contribution to staff meetings Recommendations through formal channels to improve company documentation & procedures Contribution to company website or internal magazine	
Connect & work with others	Improving work scheduling by being ready when needed Contribution to staff training programs and industry forums Flexibility when others need help or resources you control Internal networking Undertaking staff mentoring as a mentee Offering staff mentoring as a mentor Union membership & participation Engagement with staff social activities	

Recognise & utilise diverse perspectives	Recognising when other staff are struggling	
	Using formal procedures to suggest improvements	
	Participation in cultural awareness programs	
	Using language interpreting resources effectively	

If you find evidence that you have a specific core skill ... what can you do to keep it developing?

If you find little evidence that you've got it ... what can you do to get it?

This cluster of core skills is the prelude to the practical, when you have to 'get the work done' – as you'll see in the next chapter.

CHAPTER 6

Cluster Three: Get the work done

Career keywords: plan & organise; make decisions; identify & solve problems; create & innovate; work in a digital world

The five core skills in this cluster appear more concrete than the previous five, and almost look like technical skills. These are still core skills because they're about 'how' you use the technical equipment and organisational processes of your firm, and track how you contribute to their improvement.

The five core skills for this cluster are:

- Plan and organise
- Make decisions
- Identify and solve problems
- Create and innovate
- Work in a digital world

Yes ... more concrete, and I think they're getting harder! This won't be the case if you're really good at them, of course. Different people will have a different skill spread, and deep understanding and implementation capacity in only a few of the core skills. For example, you may be good at core skill five – recognise and utilise diverse perspectives. That will help you recognise this set of five core skills in others. It's a valuable skill to recognise the skills of others and partner with them to solve work problems, or prevent them.

Plan and organise

Deploying this core skill depends on your role in the organisation – more is expected the higher you rise, and a professional role will have a high level of autonomy. For example, as a career coach in private practice, it's up to me to decide what to do first – write a client report, or another chapter of my book.

With organisations doing more with less and using many automated processes, more is expected of even junior staff. You should assess the level of autonomy that you have in your role, and then rank your work tasks for importance. Some tasks are important and urgent, others are important and not urgent, others, urgent but not important, and the rest neither important, nor urgent. Check to see that your manager agrees with your ranking.

I always write my client reports first, because they're both important, and urgent.

Make decisions

Before you start making decisions, you should understand the organisational limitations – the roles, rights and responsibilities of all the people around you. You can't just pick up your phone and start barking orders.

You'll be expected to make decisions about your work within your scope, and report any unusual occurrences to your immediate manager. Sometimes this scope is well explained and documented in your job description, and sometimes just commonsense. If handling money, for example, log all invoices and receipts, even if you're not in an accounting role.

Identify and solve problems

Solving problems is part of every job – high or low. A highly programmed bank teller job should see few problems, but being the first service point in a complex system that few customers understand ensures plenty of trouble-shooting behind the counter. There will be daily opportunities to engage with customers to prevent little issues escalating.

You'll be expected to solve problems within your responsibility level, and then escalate the issue to your immediate manager within a specified time-frame. Your superior probably says, 'My door is always open. Come to me with any problems'. This really means, 'Come to me with a solution'. I've never approached a manager without bringing a solution to the problem that has arisen. I have a good example from my own career:

I once had a Career Consultant role with a large university seeing finance and management students face to face for their career development. When reviewing student resumes for graduate positions, I noticed that most had very similar resume issues at their early stages. If I saw three students over three hours, we covered the same resume issues three times.

By grouping the three students into one session and dealing with their common issues, I could save two hours of my time each day and use that to improve career seminar materials. It was a clear productivity improvement.

Fortunately, I had a resume improvement exercise that I used in my private practice, and this worked well with the students. The students rose to the occasion and were highly engaged in the resume improvement tasks in the small groups. There was no confidentiality issue, as they didn't see the other resumes during the session. After the group session, they returned for individual attention. I found I could have four students in each group, thus saving three hours a day.

After an informal trial, I took the findings to my manager who approved the new arrangement, and we advertised group sessions to students.

Create and innovate

In a 2016 article in the *Australian Financial Review*, the journalist Jennifer Gardiner stated that while Australia was number 10 on the list of countries based on success in invention, it was number 81 in applying that invention by devising real products and services. It's important nationally, and in your career, to turn invention into innovation for a productive result.

You don't have to be Einstein to create and innovate. Use the inventions of others to operationalise the improvements their inventions make possible.

Innovative implementation is an essential skill that inventors may not have themselves. This could also involve assessing new inventions for suitability to your sector. You may be working in a golf shop and have a dozen new drivers pushed on you by company reps every month. Instead of just slapping a price on these new wonders and putting them in the racks, you may take the demo clubs out for a hit and discover that the extra distance comes at the expense of accentuating your slice. By testing the inventions you can give accurate advice to club members before they spend that $499 on some graphite marvel. Part of 'create and innovate' is using your initiative to assess the inventions of others.

Thinking up a new idea is easier than implementing that idea. For information on how to do this see Chapter 10 of *The Australian Career Mentor: career guidance for experienced professionals and new graduates*. The chapter is entitled *Career confidential* and gives you an organised approach to implementing a great idea. I'm directing you to this method before you get into trouble.

This book is a good example of turning invention into reality. I wrote the *Australian Core Skills Audit,* and *The Australian Career Passport* that you'll see later in the book based on the Australian Government's *Core Skills for Work Developmental Framework*. I was impressed by the research on this new framework, and in 2013 attended the Australian Government professional development seminars. Unfortunately, it wasn't then a user-ready resource I could use with my career clients. I waited for two years for some development, but nothing happened. It appeared to be up to me to develop it – so I did! I'll let you decide if I've been successful.

Work in a digital world

This is my weakest core skill. I hope it's not yours!

Even if you're good at this, keep up to date with targeted professional development on evolving trends. If you're slipping behind, consider some short certificate courses. Many organisations have a professional development budget that can assist.

You should all know not to make derogatory comments on social media platforms about your employer or colleagues, and understand the risk you take in having your Bali Moon Party snaps available to the world. There's a trend in US hiring where candidates are asked for their Facebook passwords during the interview, so the interviewer can check them out immediately!

Skilltask 4: Got it?

Let's find some evidence that you have this cluster. In the evidence column think of your present job and keep it to small issues. For example, in 'identify and solve problems' you may have found that there were potential customers waiting outside your store 15 minutes before opening time and suggested a time change to accommodate them. You and the manager were both in the store – so why not?

Core skill	Convincing evidence	Your evidence
Plan & organise	Dealing with workload & task scheduling	
	Prioritising your tasks	
	Understanding the priorities of others	
	Linking your plans to management priorities	
Make decisions	Changing & communicating your priorities based on external developments	
	Knowing when to escalate a problem to your superior	
Identify & solve problems	Identifying equipment issues	
	Identifying process improvements	
	Identifying customer service issues	

Core skill	Convincing evidence	Your evidence
Create & innovate	Awareness of industry trends Selecting trends that could improve your productivity Integrating emerging industry knowledge into your job	
Work in a digital world	Learning to operate new programs relevant to your work	

If you find evidence that you have a specific core skill … what can you do to keep it developing?

If you find little evidence that you've got it … what can you do to get it?

This completes the core skills in action section of the book. Now that you understand them properly, and can see how they operate in the workplace, it's time to assess your skills and rank yourself.

CHAPTER 7

The Australian Career Passport

Career keywords: skills assessments; *The Australian Career Passport*; how to use the *Passport*; linking core skills to employers' needs

Now that you have a solid understanding of what core skills are and how they apply in the workplace, it's time to do an assessment to see which of these skills you have. You need to know exactly where you are with your core skills, to make better choices on future career decisions and more accurately give employers the information they're looking for.

The Australian Career Passport is based on the *Core Skills for Work Developmental Framework* developed by the Australian Government. The *Passport* tracks core skills, not technical skills. The core skills are the non-technical skills used every day to understand the workplace and negotiate with people – the oil that helps the workplace run smoothly.

How to complete the *Passport*

The Australian Career Passport enables tracking of core skills at five stages from novice performer to expert performer.

- The **novice performer (Stage 1)** has little or no practical experience in this area and is reliant on explicit rules, instructions and the guidance of others to undertake activities. *This person is focused on trying to survive.*

- The **advanced beginner (Stage 2)** has some practical experience of this skill and is beginning to recognise patterns and make connections to operate more autonomously in familiar situations. *This person is looking for certainty.*

- The **capable performer (Stage 3)** has sufficient practical experience to identify patterns and establish priorities for action and can comfortably apply the rules and work in unfamiliar situations. *This person is looking for a sense of control over events and activities.*

- The **proficient performer (Stage 4)** has considerable practical experience of this skill and can recognise patterns to respond to situations in an intuitive and flexible manner. The person may revert to analysis and seek guidance when making important decisions. *This person is starting to see the big picture.*

- The **expert performer (Stage 5)** intuitively knows what to do, can show flexibility in new situations and can change the rules to produce better outcomes for different situations. *This person understands that everything depends on the specific circumstances.*

Instructions: for each skill description, record your immediate intuitive answer by marking with a dash (-) the circle that best indicates your skill level, with Stage 1 being *'novice performer'*, and Stage 5 *'expert performer'*. If you have a skill to an expert level but don't use it often, you still are competent in that skill, so mark the 'expert performer' circle. If you feel you have no trace of a particular skill, leave that section blank.

This 12345 scale is a rough estimate, not a precise formula.

The audit is generally applicable across all occupations and sectors. There is a section at the end of each cluster allowing you or your career coach to adapt the *Passport* by adding any special non-technical skills your occupation or sector would particularly value.

Senior school students will find the ⊤ descriptors most useful. As many are working in adult environments the other descriptors may also be applicable to their situations.

Cluster 1 Navigate the world of work

Rating	Core skill description	Core skill description	Rating
5 4 3 2 1		**1. Manage career and work life** Core skill 1 means you can gain work, gain skills, do courses, keep fit with sports, balance home life ...	1 2 3 4 5
	Identify work options	***Gain work***	
00000	Understand your core skills and personal strengths	Tailor your CV and cover letter to each job application	00000
00000	Understand job ads, job descriptions and selection criteria	Write responses to selection criteria	00000
00000	Able to link your core skills, technical skills, qualifications and training to specific job ads and job descriptions	Comfortable contacting managers, HR officers and recruiters to discuss requirements for advertised positions	00000
00000	Able to manage personal life issues influencing work performance/attendance/location	Use your networking skills and strategies to tap the hidden job market	00000
		Develop a social media strategy suitable for your occupation and career stage to communicate with colleagues and potential employers	00000
00000	Know what you're good and bad at	Conduct yourself professionally during work time	00000
00000	Take part in work experience	Develop a professional brand	00000

Core skill description	Rating
Develop relevant skills and knowledge	
Identify your training and professional development needs	00000
Familiarity with the Australian Qualifications Framework	00000
Able to explore educational courses and government fee support	00000
Investigate internships and work placement programs	00000
Monitor personal/work time	00000
Able to check out careers with JIIG-CAL, www.myfuture.edu.au	00000
Understand various industries and sectors	00000
See how a specific job could advance your career interests	00000
Recognise your improvements	00000

Core skill description	Rating
Know how to assess career coaches and career programs	00000
Talk with friends about their jobs and their employers	00000
Can fill out employment application forms	00000
Comfortable approaching careers teachers	00000
Know how to contact potential employers	00000

Rating	Core skill description	Core skill description	Rating
5 4 3 2 1	**2. Work with roles, rights and protocols**	**Core skill 2 means you understand work regulations and roles, management needs, company documentation ...**	1 2 3 4 5
	Work with roles and responsibilities	**Operate within legal rights**	
00000	*Understand your work rights and obligations*	*Comply with work regulations and legal obligations of your organisation and profession*	00000
00000	*Understand pressures on your manager and work colleagues*	*Understand conflict of interest issues*	00000
00000	*Develop strategies to assist work colleagues tactfully*		
00000	*Report bullying or harassment to manager or higher authority*		
00000	*Know the rules: attendance; taking breaks; smoking*		
00000	*Know who your supervisors and managers are*		
00000	*Understand the usual practices and procedures of your team*		

Rating	Core skill description	Core skill description	Rating
00000	Follow OH&S procedures and make improvement suggestions		
00000	Understand your salary, holiday and sick leave entitlements		
00000	Report safety issues to manager immediately		
00000	Know sick leave procedures		
00000	Follow the dress standard		

Adapt the *Passport* – add your own descriptors

Rating	Personal skill descriptors	Personal skill descriptors	Rating
00000			00000
00000			00000

Cluster 2 – Interact with others

Rating	Personal skill descriptors	Personal skill descriptors	Rating
5 4 3 2 1	**3. Communicate for work**	**Core skill 3 means you listen, understand and speak in the 'culture' of the organisation...**	1 2 3 4 5
	Respond to work communication systems	*Respond to work practices and protocols*	
00000	Understand the structure of the organisation and roles of various sections	Can follow verbal and written instructions	00000
00000	Understand the meaning of organisational communications	Know how to question instructions	00000
00000	Able to complete work documentation – forms, reports, etc.	Know who to approach on particular issues	00000
00000	Complete documentation on time		
00000	Can identify different kinds of work documents – safety notices, instructions, procedures, policies	Report problems to manager	00000

Rating	Personal skill descriptors Understand, interpret and act	Personal skill descriptors Speak and listen appropriately to staff	Rating
00000	Able to provide relevant information to others when asked	Understand politeness issues with male and female peers and managers	00000
00000	Judgement on when to take action	Employ active listening to understand the needs of others	00000
00000	Understand how to clarify communication with peers	Can repair mistakes and rebuild confidence of others after personal misunderstandings	00000
00000	Understand how to clarify communication with managers		
00000	Know when to take the lead in work tasks	Know when you've made an error and apologise	00000
		Ask for explanations of industry jargon	00000
		Get the message across	
		Understand how to present opinions in work meetings	00000
		Understand meeting agendas and how to add items for discussion	00000
		Give and receive feedback appropriately and constructively	00000
		Speak publically and adjust style to audience	00000

Rating	Personal skill descriptors	Personal skill descriptors	Rating
5 4 3 2 1	**4. Connect and work with others**	**Core skill 4 means you understand strengths and weaknesses, work flexibly with others, build rapport with staff and clients...**	1 2 3 4 5
	Understand self	*Build rapport with staff and customers*	
00000	*Understand personal strengths and weaknesses*	*Understand pressures on peers and managers*	00000
00000	*Understand personal psychological style*	*Understand the issues of internal and external customers*	00000
00000	*Use intuition appropriately*	*Follow through on customer issues*	00000
00000	*Able to control personal behaviour*		
00000	*Able to get help for weaknesses*	*Greet customers appropriately*	00000
00000	*Talk with parents and careers teachers about work problems*		

The Australian Career Passport

Rating	Personal skill descriptors	Personal skill descriptors	Rating
	Cooperate and collaborate with others	**Manage conflict**	1 2 3 4 5
00000	Respond to clear requests	Understand own role& how it relates to other roles	00000
00000	Share information on relevant tasks	Develop strategies to deal with conflict	00000
00000	Follow through on commitments to peers and managers	Manage own responses to demonstrate consistent behaviours	00000
00000	Active networking	Know when to report conflict to managers	00000
00000	Participation in formal and informal mentoring relationships		
00000	Interact with multidisciplinary professionals		
00000	Give workmates help when they need it	Stay out of arguments and conflicts of other workers	00000
00000	Accept help when you need it	Keep your cool	00000
00000	Know who to ask for feedback on your performance		
00000	Understand what teamwork means on your site		

64 | Lawrence Arnold

Rating	Personal skill descriptors	Personal skill descriptors	Rating
5 4 3 2 1	**5. Recognise and utilise diverse perspectives**	**Core skill 5 means you understand manager pressures, deal with conflict, cultural and language issues, negotiate...**	1 2 3 4 5
	Recognise different perspectives	*Respond to and utilise different perspectives*	
00000	*Understand people from diverse backgrounds*	*Develop strategies to deal with differences in work style*	00000
00000	*Understand English language and literacy limitations*	*Adapt own English language(vocab and grammar) to communicate*	00000
00000	*Understand individual differences in work style and communication*	*Implement broad consultation on completing work tasks and projects*	00000
00000	*Articulate relevant personal values*		
00000	*Show respect for workers with disabilities or accents*	*Relate to people who are younger/older*	00000
00000	*Observe how managers and staff handle conflict*	*Relate respectfully to workmates of opposite gender*	00000

Adapt the *Passport* – add your own descriptors

Rating	Personal skill descriptors	Personal skill descriptors	Rating
00000			00000
00000			00000

Cluster 3 – Get the work done

Rating	Personal skill descriptors	Personal skill descriptors	Rating
5 4 3 2 1	**6. Plan and organise**	**Organise workload, prioritise tasks, work documentation, negotiate timelines ...**	1 2 3 4 5
	Plan and organise workload	***Plan and organise work commitments***	
00000	*Have personal systems to track work commitments*	*Balance own needs with those of others*	00000
00000	*Plan tasks according to unit goals and other staff*	*Establish boundaries when negotiating tasks*	00000
00000	*Take responsibility for own tasks*		
	Plan and implement tasks		
00000	*Sequence work tasks efficiently*		

Personal skill descriptors	Rating	Personal skill descriptors	Rating
Consult work guidelines on task implementation	00000		
Reassess priorities when circumstances change	00000		
Deal with unplanned events	00000		
Communicate with other staff on progress	00000		
Monitor progress against stated goals	00000		
Use appropriate tools and systems, including ICT	00000		
Persevere and maintain effectiveness under challenge	00000		
Report difficulties to manager	00000		
Follow operations manual	00000		
Keep on with positive actions when things go wrong	00000		
Report systems failures quickly	00000		

Rating	Personal skill descriptors	Personal skill descriptors	Rating
5 4 3 2 1	**7. Make decisions**	**Understand decision-making scope, review progress, report difficulties ...**	1 2 3 4 5
	Establish decision-making scope	**Apply decision-making processes**	
00000	Work within power conferred by job description and organisation's policies	Use systematic, analytical processes to make decisions	00000
00000	Take responsibility for decisions made	Use intuition appropriately	00000
00000	Involve relevant staff in collaborative decisions	Seek advice, feedback, and support as needed	00000
	✎	Consider ethical issues when making decisions	00000
00000	Know what areas of your job you can make your own decisions about	Document different tasks so others can check progress	00000
00000	Confident to ask advice from supervisor and other staff		
	Review and monitor impact of decisions		
00000	Evaluate decisions according to goals		
00000	Monitor ongoing impact of decisions		
00000	Subject decisions to formal review		

Rating	Personal skill descriptors	Personal skill descriptors	Rating
5 4 3 2 1	**8. Identify and solve problems**	**Icentify problems and solutions, review outcomes** ...	1 2 3 4 5
	Identify work problems	*Apply problem-solving processes*	
00000	Identify immediate problems	Apply standard solutions for routine problems	00000
00000	Research underlying causes and issue	Search for achievable solutions for unfamiliar problems	00000
00000	Draw on known theory for comparison	Combine intuition and analysis to devise solutions	00000
	Review outcomes		
00000	Reflect on the solution implemented for improvement		
00000	Monitor outcomes		
00000	Revise solution with emerging evidence or research findings		
00000	Investigate unintended consequences		
00000	Communicate results formally to stakeholders		

Rating	Personal skill descriptors	Personal skill descriptors	Rating
00000	Suggest operational/organisational change to prevent future issues		
54321	**9. Create and innovate**	**Seek out opportunities, develop and apply new ideas, keep up to date**	12345
	Recognise opportunities to develop and apply new ideas	***Generate ideas***	
00000	Recognise ongoing problem or processes needing change	Understand the difference between intuition and analysis	00000
00000	Test possible solutions for effectiveness	Use analysis in implementing new ideas and processes	00000
00000	Support and adopt innovative proposals by other staff	Evaluate how new ideas fit into existing products or services	00000
00000	Recognise the value of continuous improvement	Know how to pitch new ideas	00000
00000	Contribute to a culture of best practice and creativity	Aware of current industry and sector trends and experimentation	00000
		Light bulb moments – but check with others before starting	00000

Rating	Personal skill descriptors	Personal skill descriptors	Rating
	Select ideas for implementation		
00000	Use clear criteria to assess new ideas		
00000	Assess risk of new ideas that challenge existing methods		
00000	Estimate return on investment for major changes		
00000	Approach stakeholders for opinions and support		
00000	Understand organisational change implications of new ideas		
5 4 3 2 1	**10. Work in a digital world**	**Use digital technology systems in an organisational context**	1 2 3 4 5
	Use digital technologies and systems	**Connect with others**	
00000	Understand purpose of different IT programs	Know how to access help-desk support and gain informal help from colleagues	00000
00000	Select appropriate programs for specific tasks	Evaluate training programs for immediate and long-term relevance	00000
00000	Troubleshoot routine problems	Evaluate connectivity of separate platforms for work role efficiency	00000

Rating	Personal skill descriptors	Personal skill descriptors	Rating
00000	*Use digital systems to improve workplace practices*	*Assist other staff in digital improvement*	00000
00000	*Evaluate digital trends for implementation in work role*	*Membership of relevant online professional communities*	00000
		Understand and follow online etiquette	00000
00000	*Use workplace equipment and systems*		
	Access, organise and present information	**Know when to escalate problems to manager**	
00000	*Enter, store, and retrieve information and resources*		
00000	*Use digital tools to improve work efficiency*		
00000	*Integrate digital systems into work projects*		

Adapt the *Passport* – add your own descriptors

Rating	Personal skill descriptors	Personal skill descriptors	Rating
00000			00000
00000			00000

Let's check your pattern. Have you estimated a lot of core skills at 'expert' level, or not many? Most people will excel in only a few skills, so if you've ticked them all as 'high' there may be a reality problem.

Input from others

To confirm your skill levels you could try a 360 degree assessment. Ask some trusted people to evaluate you with a blank *Passport* form, then record their assessment on your form with (|), (/), and (\). If the marks all meet in the same circle, you'll have an 'asterisk of approval'. Probably, they won't all converge, and you'll have to decide who is right. If others think you don't have a high level of a particular skill, your own assessment may be wrong. Dig deep into your memory and search for evidence that you have the skill in question. Skilltasks 3, 4, and 5, have given some data to show where you excel.

You could also find someone in your workplace with a positive opinion of you, one with a neutral opinion, and one with a negative opinion, and ask them to fill out your *Passport*. This takes some courage, but will give you a rounder result.

The time machine

Most skills can be improved with time and effort ... especially effort. You may decide to work on some specific core skills, and check for improvement later. Give it six months, and do the *Passport* again to record your improvement.

Graph the grid

You can turn the information in the grid into a graph so it's easier to understand. Turn the book 90 degrees and draw a line linking all the asterisks. Do the same with the opposite column. You'll then have a visual representation of your Core Skills for Work. With 'asterisks of approval' from three other people, you can feel confident in your skills.

How to use this information

Once you've mapped your core skills you can use the information in a number of ways.

You can reflect on your core skills and accept that you're good at some things and not good at others. You can also use reflection to change your behaviour.

You can 'do', 'delegate', or 'deflect'. We all take these three approaches with different work issues at different times.

- You can 'do': You may decide that your job would run better if you could improve a specific core skill like 'identify training and professional development needs' and then investigate some appropriate courses. You could discuss this with your manager, who may have noticed areas for improvement, or talk with the HR training coordinator to see if you could attend a relevant course to improve this core skill.
- You can 'delegate': You may decide that the core skills you estimate to be at Stage 1 or Stage 2 are not very relevant to your job or career direction, and you can delegate these functions to others who would perform them better.
- You can 'deflect': You may also decide that improving greatly in these skills would be very difficult, and not worth the effort. You may make a rational decision to avoid work roles needing specific core skills, and concentrate on work roles where you show strength.

It's a high ideal to excel at everything you do, but you need to be pragmatic and make a personal business decision on the return on investment.

The correlation concept

Perhaps the most important use for this information is to prepare your future job applications, and to help you find evidence of your employability to present to employers. It's time to link your core skills with the skills employers are seeking by returning to the concept we introduced in Chapter 2 – the seven skills groups identified by the Foundation for Young Australians in online job ads.

This exercise is a 'big picture' linking of your skills and employers' needs using the information you've derived from the *Passport*. We'll fine tune this in subsequent chapters when we investigate specific work roles and job descriptions.

Skilltask 5: FYI from FYA – Core skills correlation

The aim here is to select one of the 'skills groups' you're attracted to, and then link your core skills to it.

- Use your intuition to select a skills group that attracts you.
- Check the 'snapshot of skills' to see if you're still attracted.
- Use the *Passport* to identify the core skills you have indicating compatibility with that skills group.

If you can't find much evidence from your *Passport*, maybe your intuition is poor – select again! You may also be attracted to more than one skills group. That's fine, as long as you find evidence from your *Passport* that you really do have the compatible core skills.

Skills groups	Snapshot of skills required in these groups	Snapshot of core skills you have & can demonstrate
The Generators	interpersonal interaction in retail, sales, hospitality, and entertainment	
The Artisans	skills in manual tasks related to construction, production, maintenance, and technical services	
The Carers	skills in improving the mental and physical well-being of others, including medical care and personal support	
The Coordinators	capacity to undertake repetitive administrative tasks and behind-the-scenes processes, or service tasks.	
The Designers	skills and knowledge of science, mathematics, and design to construct or engineer products or buildings	
The Informers	skills in providing information, education, or business services	
The Technologists	skilled understanding and manipulation of digital technology.	

These seven skills groups are an amalgamation of skills sought by employers. You may find that some of your strong core skills easily correlate with the skills identified in the skills snapshot column. This will give you an idea of the types of industries where your skills will be valued. This doesn't mean that other employers are no-go zones, but that you may have to investigate those employers more thoroughly to find niche positions that suit your skill set.

Now that you've narrowed down the areas where your skills appear strongly, you can start applying for specific jobs in those sectors. Target your job applications to specific employers looking for those skills, and show your skills clearly and confidently.

That's what the next part of the book is about.

Now you have formally assessed your core skills levels you'll have a database of information to assist you in applying for future jobs and planning your professional development.

PART 2

SHOW YOUR SKILLS

CHAPTER 8

Forensic investigations

Career keywords: crack the code for job descriptions; analyse selection criteria, collect evidence

In the old days of newspaper job ads, employers were brief with their words because they paid for each one. I recall a favourite TV show when I was young – 'Have Gun, Will Travel'. This was a newspaper ad meaning: 'I'm a really cool armed hit man and rights enforcer who will go anywhere in the Wild West and shoot responsibly for the appropriate fee to help virtuous lady saloon owners, defenceless widows, and crusty old guys being harassed by evil cattle barons scheming to nullify their assigned water rights'.

Today, we've moved on. With online listings, the word count is irrelevant, and you'll see long descriptions of the role and the company peppered with over-the-top phrases and poetic claims about the organisational mission. This luxury of letters should really improve communication, but it often confuses with runaway prose. Employers may know what they're looking for when they see it, but don't always say what they mean in their job ads or job descriptions. Job applicants have to 'crack the code' to see what employers are demanding for the job they've advertised.

The secret language of job ads

To help you de-code the language of job ads, let's analyse a typical online listing ad for a marketing manager role with a fictional company I'll call

Ladidas, an iconic sportswear brand. The firm is fictional but the job ad is word-for-word real.

Ladidas is a highly recognised and innovative organisation, which, with its love for sport is a major player in the industry offering a diverse range of products. Dedicated to being the best sports brand in the world, Ladidas has a continued commitment to its people and to making our superior products better. Ladidas offers much more than a job. It's where you shape the future of sport and style every day.

An exciting opportunity exists to join the Ladidas Majors team in the role of Marketing Manager Majors. This position has one direct report and is responsible for creating and implementing the strategy which drives sell-in and sell-through of Majors products and nurtures the Majors brand in the Australian Marketplace. Key elements of the role are developing communications strategies, delivering integrated Go To Market plans and ensuring the Majors brand operates at the cutting edge of marketing. This role involves both local and global travel and reports to the Marketing Director.

Key responsibilities include:
- Developing marketing strategy for the Majors brand in Australia
- Implementing ATL and BTL communications activity
- Localising marketing tools provided by Ladidas Global
- Driving innovation, particularly in digital and retail marketing
- Management of a Marketing Coordinator
- Driving agency relationships
- Working closely with the Ladidas retail team to plan and implement in-store marketing activities
- Providing post campaign analysis with a focus on ROI
- Budget management
- With category management colleagues, delivering integrated Go To Market plans to the sales and retail teams
- Developing fruitful business partnerships with key customers

- Building relationships with the Originals marketing team at Ladidas Global
- Working closely with the team manager to support the Ladidas skate team

To succeed in this role, you will need to have the following skills/ qualities/experience:

- Proven success in and a passion for sport, fashion and youth lifestyle marketing
- Deep knowledge of digital marketing trends
- A track record in thinking outside the box and delivering true marketing innovation
- Experience in managing agency relationships
- Highly developed organisational and time management skills
- Well-developed people management attributes
- Budgeting and financial management experience
- Communication & presentation expertise
- A strong working knowledge of Microsoft Office(PowerPoint, Excel, Word, Outlook)
- Willingness to travel
- Background in working for global companies is desirable

The successful candidate will be tertiary qualified in a marketing related discipline and have a strong track record as an innovative and commercially minded marketer, ideally within the sport or fashion industry. You will be capable of working autonomously, but will also be a strong team player.

If marketing is your career and sport fashion is your passion, if you are driven to innovate and you want to be part of a fast-paced and committed working environment this could be the opportunity for you.

What's on offer?

Competitive base salary, car allowance, superannuation, bonus scheme and Ladidas employee benefits for the successful candidate.

ATL means Above the Line, and BTL means Below the Line. ATL strategies in product promotion are the obvious ones like print, poster, TV and internet advertisements, where you know someone's selling you something. BTL strategies are the ones where you think you're getting information, entertainment, infotainment, or social support via an internet platform. This includes product placement – the international sports star wearing the fluoro runners and expensive watch for the press conference or talk show. Nobody is telling you to buy, but you know you could go faster with those runners, and cut your time with that watch. It also includes blogs by cool young women whose coolisity gathers an audience of 100 000 other coolettas. In a post on fitness she may just flash her new fluoro footwear. They go viral, so do sales. Marketers pay bloggers to promote products to their unsuspecting audience. BTL should be re-named BTB – Below the Belt.

While you're investigating your skills, don't forget your competitors. Check their Linkedin profiles for their evidence of their similar skills. For the Ladidas application you could type 'Marketing Manager Australia' and scroll down to 'Featured Skills & Endorsements' to see the first four keywords of the first 10-12 profiles of Australian marketing managers. Of these 50 words and phrases the most common ones are: marketing; marketing communications; marketing strategy; and online marketing (or E-commerce, digital marketing, SEO). If you add 'sportswear' into the search, two other keywords start appearing in profiles – product launch, and event management. You've just uncovered the six common keywords that insiders use to describe a high performer in this occupation.

You can now use this information in your job application by giving evidence from your career that you have these skills, by developing sentences for your resume using these keywords in your job context. When you then combine these with your core skills, you will have a powerful job application that will get through electronic gatekeeping programs, and engage the final human reader. You still may have to dig deep to find the evidence that you have this combination of technical skills and core skills, and that's why there are so many exercises in the next few pages.

Skilltask 6: Find the truffles – identifying core skills

The Ladidas ad demands a number of technical skills, core skills, and attitudes mixed together in an exciting recruiting cocktail. In this exercise, you have to separate these elements so you can address them in the job application. There are five main core skills being sought.

In the grid below, I've listed three of the five and indicated which of the core skills they're looking for with their words. You do the last two.

Ladidas demands	Corresponding core skills	The forensic evidence
'track record of thinking outside the box and delivering true marketing innovation'	Create & innovate Recognise & utilise diverse perspectives Make decisions	This ad is all about innovation and delivery within budget. You must have ideas, be able to inspire people with them, and be decisive to keep the train on track and on schedule. If you want this job, you'll have to think of several examples where you did this.
'managing agency relationships'	Connect & work with others Recognise & utilise diverse perspectives Plan & organise Work with roles, rights & protocols Communicate for work Make decisions	This bit is about managing external people that you delegate important tasks to. You will have to set up legal contracts, monitor them, and enforce them when they start failing. You will have to be very selective with the externals you contract and understand their strengths and weaknesses.
'organisational and time management skills'	Manage career & work life Plan & organise Identify & solve problems	Here, it's about prioritising competing tasks, scheduling people and the work they do. Good budget control is essential to ensure projects are delivered on time.

Ladidas demands	Corresponding core skills	The forensic evidence
You decide		
You decide		

This is quite a list of core skills but there is some overlap. Applicants wanting this job with Ladidas will have to demonstrate that they understand the demands, can link them to the core skills, and demonstrate with evidence they have the right stuff for this demanding role.

Now that you've practised extracting specific core skills from a job ad, you should now do this with a job you really want.

Skilltask 7: Target a job

Find an online job listing and fill out the grid below. In the first column enter the exact words from the job ad indicating the core skills demanded. In the second column write down the specific core skills you think are relevant. In the third column write down some keywords you would use in your resume, and job application. This is evidence that you have the core skills demanded, so it has to be true.

The target job is_____

Job demands	Corresponding core skills	Your forensic evidence

Evidence gathering

Qualifications and certificates give evidence of technical skills, but core skills are harder to assess. However, each job applicant has to provide convincing evidence for these. The following exercise will help you gather evidence from your working life to use as proof, which you can then use to address the skills identified in your target job above.

It will be useful to find evidence for skills that you think are quite weak, so all ten skills should be analysed. If you can find convincing evidence of capacity in core skills you think are weak, maybe you're not so weak in those after all. This is about evidence – not your perception. A past US president once said: 'People often misunderestimate me'. Don't you do the same.

Skilltask 8: Elementary – find the evidence

The chart below lists the ten Core Skills for Work and translates them into plain English. In the evidence column describe a situation where you demonstrated that you have this skill. Don't go for complex language here ... just put down some keywords to show you have this skill. Few people will be totally proficient in all ten skills but there should be some where you have a lot of evidence to support your proficiency.

Core skill	Plain language	Your evidence
1 - manage career and work life	Gain work in your sector, balance home life, keep fit with sports, gain skills, do some courses ...	
2 - work with roles, rights and protocols	understand work regulations, your role, the roles of others, management needs, organisational documentation ...	
3 - communicate for work	listen, understand & speak in the 'culture' of the organisation ...	
4 - connect and work with others	understand strengths & weaknesses, work flexibly with others, build rapport with staff & clients ...	
5 - recognise and utilise diverse perspectives	understand manager's pressures, deal with conflict, cultural & language issues, negotiate ...	
6 - plan and organise	organise workload, prioritise tasks, work documentation, negotiate timelines ...	

Core skill	Plain language	Your evidence
7 - make decisions	understand decision-making scope, review progress, report difficulties ...	
8 - identify and solve problems	Identify problems & solutions, review outcomes ...	
9 - create and innovate	seek out opportunities, develop/apply new ideas, keep up-to-date ...	
10 - work in a digital world	use technologies & systems, connect with others in different ways, access, organise & present information ...	

Write the Phrases: Now that you know your core skills and have evidence of your proficiency in them, you can write some sentences to show this to the employer. The more specific the better, as the employer will need to turn the page to find more evidence in your resume.

Here's an example:

Solid experience in understanding workplace regulations and making recommendations for improvement as secretary of the WHS Working Party at ABC Construction. Working Party recommendations contributed to a 5% reduction in workplace injuries over three years.

Now, you get working to develop a databank of true and verifiable statements supporting your core skills proficiency based on the keywords in each job ad.

Well-developed capacity to_____

demonstrated by_____

_____

_____

_____

Proficient in_____

shown by _____

when_____

High-level skills in_____

shown by_____

These sentences can become part of your resume skills summary, which may also include some key technical skills. You can elaborate on them in your one-page pitch or cover letter, which we'll discuss in the next chapter. They are also a good starting point to develop your interview answers.

If you've done the exercises, you'll now understand your core skills. I hope you're impressed by the person you've found. In my face-to-face job search sessions, I send my clients off for a short coffee break, and ambush them on their way back. I ask them if they'd employ the person we've revealed in our session. Would you employ you?

Now that we've cracked the code of job listings to discover the core skills employers are looking for, and learnt how to gather the forensic evidence of those, let's get into the business of how to present that evidence to a potential employer – the application process.

CHAPTER 9

The changing face of job applications

Career keywords: Unique Value Proposition; one-page pitch; hidden selection criteria

Now that you have done your forensic investigations and gathered the necessary evidence, let's look at how to present your case that you can do and will do the job, and will fit in.

The traditional job application process requires a resume, cover letter, and responses to selection criteria, as three separate documents. While a time-consuming process for both parties, the expectations are clear:

- the resume is about the applicant, but also works on the employer's pain points;
- the responses to selection criteria provide evidence of the skills needed to undertake the position; and
- the cover letter concentrates, not on repeating the selection criteria, but on presenting evidence that the applicant can undertake the duties of the position.

These three documents must be able to stand alone, but also reinforce each other to provide a neat triangulated package impelling the employer to interview you.

There are many employers still requiring this traditional framework, but there are also employers using a more streamlined process. The new checklist for your job application includes your:

- resume tailored to the job description;
- one-page pitch;
- completed online job application form;
- answers to online questions/video interviews; and
- supporting documents you may be able to attach.

Don't blow your chances of getting the job before you even send your application. Read the employer's application instructions carefully and submit the exact mix of documents specified. Each of these should support your Unique Value Proposition. Because your Unique Value Proposition is integral to the process, let's look at how to develop that before looking at the other documents in more detail.

Your Unique Value Proposition

Many applicants have similar qualifications, so demonstrating some unique skills or work experience relevant to the employer's needs will set you apart. If the job is junior and simple, it could be 'able to take any shifts, any days'. For young people, flexibility and reliability are key must-haves. For professional positions, it's more than just being there. This Unique Value Proposition is your special claim to the job, but needs to be as much about the employer as about you. You need to find a way to make that clear.

I'll give you an example from my own career:

> For over 12 months up to May 2009, I was a member of a team developing the 2009 Career Development Association of Australia national conference in Melbourne. We'd meet every month to develop the conference theme and plan specific sessions and activities. We got to know each other quite well over that time. Quite a few people dropped out for various reasons, and the conference coordinator and I were the only ones who started together and finished together a year later.
>
> One new member who'd joined six months into the process was the manager of a university Graduate Careers Centre. At one of the last

team meetings, she asked us if we knew of a qualified career counsellor who'd be interested in taking a part-time position in her unit, to free her up for high-level meetings involving a complex inter-organisational amalgamation. I rang the next day to express my interest.

I underwent a traditional selection process – resume, cover letter, responses to selection criteria, reference checks, two interviews, and a presentation. After I'd accepted the offer, the manager even asked permission to call my previous manager at Monash University for a final check! HR could see that she wasn't just hiring one of her mates, but a highly skilled person who'd gone through a proper recruiting procedure.

Throughout the selection process, I presented my Unique Value Proposition that I had held a similar position with a similar university, and that I could demonstrate a successful career as an organisational change consultant with high-profile organisations. This combination made me unique amongst other applicants. While not expecting to be involved in the amalgamation operationally, my unique experience represented added value to a manager in having a staff member who had been through the experience of organisational change several times, and who might have access to under-the-table resources to support the difficult transition. I was originally supposed to be there 'just till the students left at the end of the year', but my contract was extended several times because of the unique value that I added to the role.

My Unique Value Proposition could be stated as:

As well as having the knowledge and skills to carry out the duties of the position successfully, I have also had the experience of holding organisational change positions previously. As set out in my attached resume, I have held three such positions and in each role contributed to the successful change envisaged. On a personal level, these roles helped me develop the professional judgement needed to steer organisations through challenging times and help colleagues deal with difficult situations.

In demonstrating skills beyond the job description, my manager knew I could have been called on for extra assistance. After a couple of months the amalgamation stalled, and later, it collapsed totally.

Skilltask 9: Your Unique Value Proposition

You need to define your Unique Value Proposition considering the needs of the employer and then demonstrate that some skills, attributes, or experience will help with a specific issue confronting the employer.

Crack the code for the job you chose last chapter, and then link your relevant skills to the job demands.

Job demands	Your relevant skills	Your unique value

Now that you know how to pinpoint your Unique Value Proposition, let's go on and look at how to put together the paperwork for your job application.

Your one-page pitch

As discussed, the job application process is becoming more streamlined, and the one-page pitch is replacing the cover letter and the responses to selection criteria document. This is not just my view – it comes from the top! At a national level, the Australian Government is altering its recruitment approach to search for people who can demonstrate more global skills, not just technical ones. Complex selection criteria are out – replaced with a resume and a 'one-page pitch'. The 2015 Department of Prime Minister and Cabinet communiqué states: 'We've replaced Public Service jargon and Duty Statements with inspiring job ads that tell candidates who we are, what we do, what we're trying to achieve, and what opportunities we offer'. Many job applicants will have difficulty with this new approach and will struggle to crack the code – but not you!

We know how long a one-page pitch should be ... but what goes into it?

With the moving sands of Australian recruitment, you need a basic road map. Let's get back to basics on this, and review the recruitment mantra.

- Can the person do the job?
- Will the person do the job?
- Will the person fit in?

Your resume (more about this in the next chapter) has a lot of information about your technical skills and core skills, but the one-page pitch uses the bare bones of what the employer wants. You need to pique interest. Your aim is for the employer to be engaged by your pitch, seek fuller information in your resume and supporting documents, and then call you. The rest is history.

For the pitch, I suggest slightly altering the recruitment mantra order above. Start by showing you have the enthusiasm and motivation to do the job (will do), indicating that you understand the job, and will take the job, if offered. Then deploy some statements demonstrating that your relevant skills ensure you know how to do the job (can do). Finally, give evidence that you can fit into the role and organisation (will fit). Because this is a new text type (trust me, I'm an Applied Linguist!) you can ditch the old letter formalities and be more adventurous in how you express yourself. This is what a fictional person called Kim Lee did when writing a one-page pitch for the Ladidas job from the previous chapter. You'll see the everlasting elements of human communication coming through ... the 6Ws – who, what, when, where, how, and the most important ... why. That is, 'why' the applicant should get an interview.

Kim Lee Application for Ladidas Marketing Manager, Majors

I'm applying for the position of Ladidas Marketing Manager, Majors because I use the gear, value the quality, and am prepared to pay the price. Also, I've just returned from two years in Europe where I was a marketing operative for Mike *NOW!* competing head to head with the Majors range. I reported directly to the Mike *NOW!* Marketing Manager, and subbed for him in meetings which he often delegated to me.

I coordinated our consumer focus groups and analysed the data obtained to determine Mike *NOW!* products, positioning, pricing, and promotion. I used my creative and innovation skills in getting the results. I harnessed the diverse perspectives of the marketing team by motivating and mentoring less experienced staff members. I worked with different organisational roles to understand their competing priorities and tied my unit's operational needs to them to get us all working together.

We developed insights into how to extend Mike positioning to tap into the new market of young people moving into parenthood who wanted to keep their association with the Mike *NOW!* range, and extend it with new children's products. I was at the product development centre of the Mike Mini *ME!* range of kidswear that mirrored our female buyer's style and colours. I feel confident to undertake similar research in the Australian market to expand the Majors brand presence, and get product to market before the Mike *NOW!* range hits here.

Part of my role was developing, and evaluating ATL and BTL strategies for ROI. I initiated and implemented the Mike *NOW OR NEVER!* campaign that used an unusual BTL strategy to deliver high ROI by placing the brand in a new consumer segment. Tapping this new segment added GBP 1.3 million over the triennium. I feel I can do the same for Ladidas Majors in Australia.

I've got all the skills needed – marketing qualifications, data analysis of focus group information, staff supervision, and liaison with agencies and external consultants. With Mike *NOW!* I did a lot of the budget work that resulted in successful marketing campaigns brought in on budget, and within the strict seasonal time frames.

I'd like to talk about the possibilities and am available for interview at a mutually convenient time. Contact: klee123@gmail.com and 0449 444 999. I'm keen to get started.

Kim Lee
June 5, 2016

Skilltask 10: Analyse the pitch

Circle the parts of Kim's pitch that 'will do', 'can do', and 'will fit'. What is the Unique Value Proposition? Why would Ladidas be interested in this?

_____

_____

_____

_____

_____

_____

_____

_____

_____

_____

_____

_____

_____

_____

_____

_____

Skilltask 11: Your Pitch Plan

Now you've seen how to write a pitch, do one for a job you really want. Take that job you targeted in Skilltask7. Underline all the keywords and then compare them with the core skills from your *Passport* to check you have the skills needed. If so, do this exercise. If not, apply for a different job.

In the 'keywords' column, list the job description keywords and phrases that correspond to the recruiting mantra at the left. Then do the same with your technical skills and core skills. If you have a lot of blank spaces and you're struggling to make the case, this may not be the job for you. Once you've linked the recruiting mantra, the job ad keywords, and your skills, this is your writing plan enabling you to produce the phrases for your pitch.

Your Pitch Plan	Job description keywords	Technical skills & core skills	Your pitch phrases
Will do the job			
Can do the job			
Will fit in			

Now, write the one-page pitch for that job you really want.

Hidden selection criteria

Because the old practice of submitting a 'Responses to selection criteria' is out and the selection criteria are now being addressed in a one-page pitch, you probably won't be able to cover all of them. Make a decision on the most important keywords, and concentrate on those. You're better to cover a smaller number with some supporting evidence than deal with the whole lot superficially by making unsubstantiated assertions.

While selection criteria are usually given to you up front, you also need to be aware of any 'hidden' selection criteria, and also address those in your pitch. This will put you a step ahead of your competitors, so let's have a look at how to uncover these hidden gems.

The Ladidas job description lists publically the skills/qualities/experience needed for the job, and you should be able to demonstrate the most important. However, there may be some skills that are really important to the manager, but that may not be mentioned – the hidden selection criteria.

Most managers use intuition as well as rationality – I do!

I once managed a team of five, delivering complex projects with differing resources on different time scales. We'd had the sudden resignation of a project manager, and discovered she'd left a key task unfinished before leaving. She'd told us a large budget item had been dealt with, but we discovered this wasn't true when the accountant checked her project. Others wanted to get out the posse, but I told everyone to move on, and that a key skill we'd need from her successor would be 'emergency trouble-shooting'. How could you put that story in a professional job description? It was my 'hidden selection criterion' – someone with an assertive personality to deal with emergencies without needing my daily supervision.

We knew we had two good 'can do', 'will do', 'will fit' applicants. One was a fully qualified person with a clear track record in the area. Everything about Michelle was good. The other person was William – no relevant qualification, but older, wiser, and politely assertive. I knew this because he was a consultant who'd approached us earlier for some specific information. I'd offered to give him the information on our district – and he asked for the whole state! This was information in the public domain, so I gave it to him. That's the attitude I needed for the job. I decided we had to have him. We hired him – and he was better at the job than I was!

But, how do you discover the hidden selection criteria before you put in the application? You track down the line manager by phone, and follow Kim's lead.

'Hello Mr Dreadnought. My name's Kim Lee and reception put me through about the marketing manager position. I'm just applying, and have followed the selection criteria in the job description. I was wondering if there's anything else I need to know before I send in my application.'

'Yes, Kim. We've had some applications in already. Could you tell me a bit about yourself? And call me Brendan.'

'Sure Brendan. I'm a marketing professional, just back from London where I worked on the Mike NOW! range, and developed a new below the line marketing strategy that my boss bought into, and we thought was pretty successful. It was 1.3 million over three years – and that was pounds.'

'Yes, Kim, that got a bit of coverage even down here. OK, we need all the stuff in the ad, but the key thing I'm looking for is someone who can connect with new communities of buyers. And I mean community seriously. It's not just about selling runners. You know the history of Ladidas, and after the war, it saved a community – just like Mike. So you know we mean it. I need someone who can connect with the community, not just sell runners. We'll get applicants with MBAs, MBBs, and MBbloodyCs, but I want someone who's serious about the community ... and fun too! It's got to be fun for the buyers, and us. I also need someone who can communicate these values to the younger staff. They think I'm some old hippy, just like their parents. But these values are important, and I want them to get it. I don't know if that makes any sense to you, Kim.'

'Thank you, Brendan, it does. Mike in Germany started on the other side of the river to Ladidas, and we have parallel values. That's what I liked

about Mike in London. I hope to bring that to a new role. You've given me a lot of help today, so thank you very much.'

'That's great, Kim. Sorry, I get a bit worked up on this. I'll look forward to seeing your application.'

Sure, a contrived conversation, but all my clients do this – successfully. You'll be astounded at what managers tell a total stranger over the phone, once they vet you – which they can easily do with the phone in one hand and the other searching online for your Linkedin profile.

Skilltask 12 Change Kim's application

You now know the hidden selection criteria for the Ladidas position. Circle any parts of the pitch that address the 'hidden selection criteria' that are not detailed in the job description, but that may influence the hiring decision. Is there anything you'd change about the pitch?

_____

_____

_____

_____

_____

_____

_____

_____

_____

The one-page pitch uses the public and hidden information to influence the employer to interview you. It's supported by the most important document ever written – your resume.

Implementing the techniques in this chapter will ensure your application meets current expectations and practices, is compelling, and accurately targets the job in question.

CHAPTER 10

The most important document ever written

Career keywords: Professional profile; resume billboard; career achievements; Applicant Tracking Systems

The resume is the most important document most people ever write, but there's dispute on how long it should be, what should be in it, how to format it, or how to use it. We don't even have an English word for it! 'Curriculum vitae' is a Latin phrase meaning 'the course of your life', and 'resume' is a French word. We use the two terms interchangeably, but they're technically quite different.

The 'curriculum vitae' is a listing of your major career positions so the reader can investigate you thoroughly. This form is appropriate only for academic or very senior management positions. In Australia, the shorter 'resume' is preferred.

The aim of the resume is to get you the interview. It's a marketing document that you tailor to each job application and each employer. Everything in your resume must be true and, preferably, verifiable. You shouldn't put everything in this document – only that which is relevant to the job, or gives context to your career narrative. Here's a sample resume.

Kim Lee   **Marketing Manager, Majors**

klee123@gmail.com
0449 444 999

Professional profile

Experienced marketing professional with post-GFC international track record of adding GBP 1.3 million to Mike *NOW!* sales by applying tough ROI expectations on marketing creativity when using an innovative BTL strategy to tap new market segments. Keeping the respect of young customers through communicating value via a range of platforms and personal interactions leading to strong corporate branding. Managing high-level liaison with agencies and internal associates resulting in the satisfaction of seeing Go To Market plans succeed in the real world and derive accurate customer data to make superior products better.

Key skills

- Developing creative, innovative, and effective BTL strategies that don't 'talk down' to customers, resulting in product growth beyond the advertising budget
- making tough decisions by using ROI statistics to expand or terminate sales campaigns
- connecting and working with team members through mentoring to build on their existing technical skills to improve their connections with others
- high-level communication skills gaining the trust of focus groups so they give accurate product and sales campaign evaluations
- tapping new market segments in their normal environment with fun and experiential sports-related merchandising strategies for people who don't usually do sports

- understanding different roles and priorities in evaluating appropriate agencies for specific marketing strategies resulting in effective marketing campaigns with high ROI

Employment experience

Assistant Marketing Manager, Mike *NOW!* London UK   2013 – 2016

The Mike *NOW!* key marketing priority from 2014 onwards was tapping the new market segments of young parents buying for kids, and international university and college students seeking fashionable and affordable style statements.

Responsibilities: developing marketing strategies with the marketing manager; assembling and facilitating new product focus groups; budgeting for focus groups; customer interaction at university and polytechnic sports activities; liaison with agencies

Achievements:

- initiating and monitoring an innovative BTL strategy tapping new market segments that improved sales by GBP 1.3 million over the triennium but that didn't look pushy to young customers
- developing a team of product ambassadors on university campuses to promote our products at sports events thus building consumer trust and brand loyalty
- selecting focus group members across the country based on accurate demographic research
- strong liaison with management accounting staff to track ROI for marketing and merchandising campaigns

Marketing Assistant, Australian Wine Group, UK 2009 – 2013

AWG goals were to survive the GFC by changing product range, and radically altering pricing/marketing strategy.

Responsibilities: developing marketing strategies with the marketing manager; assembling and facilitating focus groups to determine new range product pricing; liaison with agencies and product distribution network

Achievements:

- expanding focus groups to new regional cities for the new wine range
- improving focus group questioning and price rating exercises
- developing a new merchandising strategy based on focus group research that increased AWG revenue by 5% annually in difficult trading circumstances
- initiating a social media strategy 'acquire affordable Australia' positioning AWG product as an affordable luxury during the GFC
- increasing AWG revenue by targeting distributer agreements on differential pricing for company functions

Marketing Assistant, Gridlock Sportswear, Melbourne 2006 – 2008

The Gridlock Sportswear strategic goal during this period was to consolidate the product distribution network, and open up new direct distribution avenues.

Responsibilities: assembling and assisting with new product focus groups; administration of focus group process; product presentation to focus groups; liaison with advertising agencies and distributors

Achievements:

- targeting local sports teams' practice evenings and taking stock to them
- initiating merchandising days for women's sports teams called 'Give him one, too', increasing annual revenue by 4%

Community

Volunteer, Melbourne Buggy Mothers Mini-Marathon 2016

A non-competitive, fun, community health event targeting 'Buggy Mothers' to improve their health, fitness, and community involvement. I was on the committee developing the pre-event fitness preparation notes, and marketing strategy. I developed a 'proportional pricing' policy entry fee linked to the distance participants estimated they could handle to attract a wide range of fitness levels. We had 240 mothers with buggies running and walking the event, and a team of 28 handling the logistics. The organising committee doubled after the event.

Referees

Mr John Smith
Marketing Manager
Mike *NOW!*
smithj@markmikenow.com
0337 445 566

Ms Janice Hua
Marketing Coordinator
M&X International
janicehua@mandx.com
0889 776 655

While it's standard to place the referees' details across the page to save space, this may 'confound the ATS' and result in contact information being confused in the database. This may prevent an automated call program (or an unautomated junior intern) from contacting your referees. There's a full discussion on ATS in Chapter 12.

Now, let's break down Kim's resume and look at the individual elements in more detail.

What's in a name?

Quite a lot apparently! Is Kim Lee male or female, young or old, Australian born or not ... and does it make any difference in getting an interview?

There's been some Australian National University research on how much having an 'ethnic' name changes the interview call rate for people with similar qualifications and experience. The researchers submitted 4000 applications for hospitality industry positions advertised online – sending the same resumes but with altered names. Chinese name resumes had to be submitted 68% more than Anglo name resumes to be considered for interview. Arabic name resumes were submitted 64% more, and Italian name resumes only 7% more. It seems that Australian employers have faith in the cosmic link between Italian name coffee and Italian name baristas! Is this racism, or coffeeism? There's a perception amongst employers that people further away from an 'Australian' background would have lower employability in the hospitality industry. While this view persists, they will continue to have lower employment!

People traditionally alter their names on their resumes to fit in better. I recall one young man who'd altered his Chinese name to Richard Trelawny-Sympson in the ultimate re-vamp. I told him he'd been watching far too much *Downton Abbey*, and we came to a more credible compromise. I suggest choosing an alteration you're already using socially, and close to the sound of your real name. There's no issue with original immigration documentation, as employers will understand when they see your passport and visa details.

It's your decision to alter a birth name – you've changed a name, not your personality, or your family.

Resume billboard

Your professional profile and your key skills summary make up the billboard on the first half page. If this is targeted, strong, and engaging, the

Skilltask 13: Probing the profile

The professional profile should use relevant keywords, and answer the 6Ws – who?, what?, when?, where?, how?, and why?? Review the professional profile in the Kim Lee resume and fill in the grid below.

6Ws	Information from Kim Lee professional profile
Who ... is Kim? background; attitudes; special attributes; motivations	Why is this information significant for the Ladidas job?
What ... was achieved? achievements; projects; qualifications; networks; insights	Why is this information significant for the Ladidas job?
When ... was it achieved? time frame; recent or remote; industry context; economic situation	Why is this information significant for the Ladidas job?
Where ... was it achieved? local/international; cultural context; target groups	Why is this information significant for the Ladidas job?
How ... was it achieved? methods; skills; style; relationships	Why is this information significant for the Ladidas job?
Why ... would you interview Kim?	

Further information on how to structure your professional profile to achieve a similar result may be found at pages 116 – 121 of *The Australian Career Mentor: career guidance for experienced professionals and new graduates.*

Does *your* professional profile provide the 6Ws?

employer will check out the rest of your resume for the evidence to prove your assertions. The call to interview is inevitable.

Now, put yourself in the position of the Ladidas HR professional and inspect Kim's resume for congruence. Find evidence to support the statements in the professional profile. Also search for any contradictory information. Is there anything to cause concern? Are there any questions you'd like to ask Kim at the interview?

You may think that Kim's professional profile is over the top, but I guarantee it will secure the interview. The less your profile looks like Kim's, the less I guarantee the outcome!

Professional experience

Your professional experience presentation should follow a pattern.

- First, state the organisational context of your role. If the Global Financial Crisis, a major merger with another business, or the sudden replacement of the Managing Director had affected the business, then make this clear in the brief business description section. **Use keywords.**
- Second, list your key responsibilities in short phrases across the page. Most HR people already know what the job 'does', so don't waste space with extensive dot points pasted from your present job description. **Use keywords.**
- Third, dot point your achievements in each role. This is what employers want to focus on. They know you turned up every day, but did you actually achieve anything? **Use keywords.**

Kim's resume deals with these three points.

Don't underestimate the importance of context, as it shows your motivation to do the job. I once had a client we'll call Ali who came for the Interview Skills Program:

Ali was a doctor who had performed surgery in a war zone before coming to Australia and working in metropolitan hospitals. He wanted to improve his interview presentation for the Royal Australian and New Zealand College of Surgeons Surgical Education and Training program.

In his war zone context, he'd performed surgery with a diminishing medical cabinet, power outages, and cruise missiles coasting along the boulevards. I think I'd like my surgeon to be able to cope with a high environmental stress level as well as being able to cut a curved line.

I hope that when I have some emergency surgery, there's someone like Ali standing at the end of the bed holding the chart when I come around.

In the new context of a well-equipped hospital and a safe environment, this great doctor will be even more outstanding. Showing the context of previous successes gives an employer confidence of future successes in the new work situation.

reverse chronological

ATS

6Ws

What?

Where?

Who?

How?

keywords in context

Why?

When?

the robots

achievements

responsibilities

the resume billboard

key skills

Skilltask 14: Achieving achievements

Knowing how to present your achievements using job ad keywords in simple dot points is ... an achievement. Let's practise it here.

The reader wants to know what you did, how you did it, and the result in the context of the time and the circumstances of particular employers. Use this pattern to write your dot point sentences demonstrating your achievements.

Achieving something in difficult circumstances shows your resilience. With better resources you'll achieve even more. Your sentences here will be similar to the ones you wrote in the 'Crack the Code' exercise earlier, but should provide fuller information.

Think of one of your recent achievements and use the pattern to present it clearly to the reader.

What you did	I ...
How you did it	I ...
The result	The result was ...

Now, you have to condense it all down into a neat package of one or two sentences. Use strong action verbs to convey your actions – coordinated, managed, initiated, consulted with, etc.

Now write your achievement succinctly:

_____

_____

_____

_____

_____

The student resume

Your resume is easier, and there's a lot of support to help you write a good one. Parents often call me wanting to book in their children for career coaching. I usually tell them to save their money, and consult the school careers teacher. They can show you great online career resources like www.myfuture.edu.au and programs like JIIG-Cal that have been designed for your age group. There will be career lessons, and a work experience program.

Hobsons, the big educational publishers, produces *The Good Careers Guide* with clear job profiles, and *The Good Universities Guide* compares universities and higher education providers. Online versions are at www. hobsonscoursefinder.com.au .You can also go to any of the universities, find their careers centre and use the materials there – anybody can just wander in and use the resources.

You can attend career expos. There are two big ones in Melbourne each year, and the major cities have similar events. There are some employers there, but it's mainly TAFEs and universities promoting their courses.

> *Ben and his girlfriend both went to the Melbourne Career Expo when he was in first year uni, and she was finishing Year 12. It was huge. They even had McDonald's doing free coffees – and they were good.*
>
> *They brought their resumes and lined up for the free resume review. It was early in the day, and a bit quiet, so the career counsellor gave them some extra time. He usually works in the city seeing a lot of finance and banking employees.*
>
> *He was really impressed with their aim to spend a year in Brazil with a conservation foundation. He was a bit concerned at two young people hacking off into the jungle, but saw they'd found a legit organisation that does these international exchanges. Prince William did one! The counsellor suggested taking a gap year. Ben could apply any time, and the girlfriend could defer her place as soon as offered. The parents were happy with their kids going off together into the jungle (that's what they said anyway). They're just good friends – it's not some big romance.*
>
> *The exchange foundation is monitoring the Amazon dolphins, so both their skills in marine biology and genetics would be useful (she's interested in genetics). The counsellor really liked her personal profile. He said it conveyed her energy and enthusiasm that she'd need to get through a challenging year away from home. This is it:*
>
> > *Because I'm interested in science and the natural environment, I'm enthusiastic about joining an environmental organisation that can do some good. I have good scientific research skills, as well as the determination and rigour to push through problems for a result. I work well with other people and was awarded a National Science Project Award with my team for our project*

Water Health of Melbourne's Eastern Streams and Creeks. I want to make a difference – and I will.

Ben's was good too, and he'd used The Australian Career Passport *to present his skills well. The counsellor recognised Ben from Nextdoor, and said it would be interesting to be changing his 'career identity' from soapie star to David Attenborough! He wanted to use it as an example in his next career book. He was really interested in how Sasha Stardust handled all the publicity, and Ben told him how down to earth she really was. The media gets her wrong.*

The career counsellor could see that Ben's career could take a few different paths, and it would be difficult to predict what would happen. In fact, they both have great futures ahead, and they seemed to be developing a great partnership; a professional partnership – it's not some big romance.

Now, write your personal profile here, and then put it at the top of your resume just under your name and contact details. See the Kim Lee resume, but yours will be less complex.

ATS alert

The Applicant Tracking System revolution is disturbing everybody. I'm less concerned, because paradoxically it brings back good resume writing. In the ATS cosmos, resume writing has to be thoughtful, disciplined, and targeted at an audience for an outcome – like any good writing. I accept that many people don't have the high-level writing skills to be successful in this. That's OK, as many professional resume writers don't have these skills either! It'll take a lot of professional development to become highly proficient in writing your resume. I've undertaken that professional development, so here are some tips and pointers to contend with the ATS, not confound it:

- Submit your resume in Word format. Never use a PDF file, as it won't be read by many ATS systems. This is because ATS parses your resume content – breaking it down into storable chunks of linked and integrated phrases clustering around the keywords it's seeking. Beautifully presented graphics and photographs can't be parsed for meaning, and the whole resume will be unreadable – **robotic rejection.**
- Don't submit electronic resume templates available on the internet or from resume services. Some ATS programs won't read templates – **robotic rejection.**
- Information in headers and footers like your name and contact details may not be read – **robotic rejection.**
- Cluster your contact details at the top left of the resume, but no personal address. If visa status is an issue, then include 'Australian PR' or such, in this section.
- On the top right include the exact job title of the position, otherwise the robot won't know which job you're applying for – **robotic rejection.**
- Use a standard font consistently throughout. Different fonts and italics may confound the ATS, which may not know where things begin and end. Use 10 – 14 throughout. Too small and too large may confound the ATS – **robotic rejection.**
- Resume length is irrelevant for the ATS, but the human reader still won't read excessively long content. If you can't get an interview

with an engaging professional profile, a targeted key skills summary, and achievements in a couple of recent relevant positions, you won't get it with some old job you listed on page five.

- Use traditional headings, like Professional Profile and Key Skills. ATS won't recognise Magic Mushroom Manipulations or other non-standard headings, so won't download your content into the database. Similarly with your job titles – use standard titles, not whacky ones like Senior IT Genius. Change it to IT Support Consultant.

- Nouns are more searchable than verbs because the human setting up the database fields tends to enter nouns rather than verbs. Sophisticated ATS software will parse the root of either, but your employer may have an older system. An old resume writer trick is to use an action verb in one sentence and then ensure the corresponding noun is used (in context!) in the next line e.g. 'organising teams within IBM to develop ...' , and in the next sentence, 'The organisation of relevant teams resulted in ...'

- Dot points are fine, but use the same size and alignment consistently. The sub, and sub-sub dot points favoured in IT resumes may confound the ATS and result in information being downloaded into the inappropriate database field. When the human searches for X, your Y will come up. The human reader will probably not investigate further, but just move on to the next applicant – **robotic rejection.**

- Lines may confound the ATS, and prevent your good content being downloaded – **robotic rejection.**

- Boxes, grids and tables may confound the ATS, so should never be used. Human readers like tables for clarity, but robots get confused and don't download the content – **robotic rejection.**

- Extend sentences to the edge of the margins, if possible as a lot of white space may confound the ATS – **robotic rejection.**

- Keywords in context derived from the job description or job ad are essential. Ensure that keywords are included in content rich sentences, so the ATS doesn't reject you for gaming the system. The context substantiates the skills and experience you are claiming. Without a convincing context – **robotic rejection.**

- Ensure you have a reverse chronological listing of your previous positions. This narrative convinces the ATS that you have held relevant positions, and gained the relevant experience needed in those. You should keep the job titles consistent with the conventional expectations of the ATS. If some previous organisations have used unusual job titles, change them to the usual industry standard. You can explain this in the interview, but may not get one if the ATS can't read a developing narrative with progression from junior positions to your present role – **robotic rejection**.

- Do mention iconic organisations, if possible, as ATS searches for these to download.

- While tedious, it's safer to list each position with the same company as though it's a separate job. The ATS doesn't understand anything, so can't separate out all these positions to download them into the database. If this is lengthening the resume excessively, maybe you shouldn't be going back so far. Anything beyond five years is hard to justify. If you're demonstrating a skill used twenty years ago ... maybe you haven't used it in the last five years. Compounding several positions into one generic section will confound the ATS – **robotic rejection**.

- Include referees, because of the ATS revolution. If the human database developer has opened a referee field you must sow your seed in it! List referees down the page, not across it. It looks like a waste of space, but if the ATS confuses the names with each other – **robotic rejection**.

These ATS essentials will reduce the chance of immediate rejection.

Targeting your resume and keeping the ATS robots happy will ensure you have the best chance of getting through the application process to the interview.

CHAPTER 11

Jump the job queue

Career keywords: hidden job market; the return of the phantom; targeted hidden job market strategies; Employee Referral Program; Linkedin profile; networking card; elevator pitch

So far we've looked at how to incorporate your core skills into the application process for advertised jobs. But as we all know, some jobs are not advertised. This chapter is going to look at how to work the 'hidden' job market, and how to get your networking tools up and running so you can be ready to pounce the moment you uncover that hidden gem of a job.

Light on the hidden job market

The 'hidden job market' is the name given to all the unadvertised jobs out there. If you contact the employer before the job is advertised, you're ahead. Even though you're the only applicant you'll still need to send this contact an outstanding resume, and a one-page pitch targeted to the business needs of the firm.

There's no doubt that the hidden job market exists. The only argument is the size, as this indicates the amount of time you should spend trying to access it.

You'll have heard statements like: 'Only 20% of jobs are ever advertised'. I've even heard 10%, and I recently saw one US article stating that only 5%

of jobs are advertised, and these are the worst jobs – that's why employers have to advertise them.

The good news is – this isn't true.

The best way to estimate the size of the hidden job market is to ask employers the sources of hire of their new employees. The Department of Employment interviewed 10 000 employers in 2016 to gather this information for their *Employers' Recruitment Experiences* report, concluding that 'about one third of jobs are not formally advertised'. This busts the 80% myth! This data indicates you should be applying aggressively for the 70% of jobs that are advertised on internet job boards, company websites, in newspapers, by recruiters and job agencies in their openly available job listings.

The report states that 17% of vacancies are filled by word of mouth – mainly in regional areas, and for lower-level jobs. In 13% of vacancies, 'employers consider job seekers who approached them about potential vacancies', but there's no indication that those who approached got those jobs. If we take out some percentage points for that, we get close to my estimate that the hidden job market is about 25%. The Australian Government statistics may surprise you, as they contradict everything you've ever been told, so I've included them in Appendix B.

So, spend 80% of your job search time researching the majority of jobs that are openly advertised, or actively promoted to the appropriate target group. It's still worth spending 10-20% of your time going after the hidden jobs, as the hidden job market certainly exists (I've been a beneficiary of it many times). I recommend 10-20% because by using the strategies in this book you're increasing your chances of success in the 'open' job market.

Many career coaches push the hidden job market concept and assure you they have the secret key to open the spectral door, but I think you already have that key – with a concept we've already discussed!

The return of the phantom

This hidden job underworld is where the biblical concept of Chapter 1, your employability, comes back to haunt you, or save you. Your high career identity ensures you're easy to find; your high personal adaptability ensures you're easy to hire; and your high human and social capital ensure you're worth hiring! With high employability, the hidden job market miraculously will find you, but you should also be pro-active in deploying selected strategies.

Hidden job market strategies

Cold calling is the technique that most people think of first when it comes to the hidden job market. It consists of walking the streets with a dozen copies of your resume, or sending unsolicited prospecting emails to hundreds of possible employers. Not surprisingly, cold calling has a success rate of less than 1%, so you're better spending your time on job search activities with a better return on investment – including submitting high-quality applications for advertised vacancies. Mix up your strategies and favour the ones that seem to be getting you closer to interviews, and offers. Try implementing a strategy for as long as you can take it, and then do something else. It depends on your personality, as one of my young clients, we'll call Elise, found out:

Elise had just completed her accounting master degree, and wanted to be pro-active in her job search. She was keen to try some cold calling, and had come to me for some appropriate strategies. I gave her the cold-calling stats, but I could tell she really wanted to try it out. She saw it as a 'Rite of Passage' to becoming a job seeker.

Her strategy was to draw a spiral out from her house and visit every accounting practice and small business in this exponentially expanding zone. She'd be in her business suit with her new resume. I wasn't convinced she'd have the energy to stick at it too long, but gave her some cunning tips to get past the receptionists and engage the accounting professional working away in the back. I wished her well and off she went.

She called me three weeks later, telling me she'd been successful in getting an offer as an assistant accountant. She was really happy, as was I. The success wasn't due to cold-calling. She'd been very consistent in her strategy, but had also applied for an advertised vacancy with a small firm three suburbs away. She wouldn't have been scheduled to visit this firm until after they'd appointed their new junior accountant – Elise!

Another hidden job market strategy often promoted is enlisting everybody you know in your job search – family, friends, people at the gym, tennis club, golf club, the casino... While this taps your social capital, you may find the scattergun approach unsuccessful. Most people won't have a job for you, and the message of the kind of job you really want may not get through clearly. Your helpers may promote your finance and banking experience to firms that construct river levee banks. There may be social pressure to take a position that doesn't suit you. If you reject offers, people won't risk helping you again. You don't want people at the golf club jumping into the bunkers every time you walk by. That really would limit your social capital. Separate your personal and professional networks.

Rather than focusing on low-ROI techniques, devote more time to incorporating sensible hidden job market strategies into your job search. The aim of these strategies is to get you into the same space as industry employers, or the people who could introduce you to them. Such strategies would be:

- attending career expos and talking with employer representatives;
- attending job fairs at your tertiary institution, and visiting the careers centre;
- volunteering for your professional association's state or national conference;
- perfecting your Linkedin profile to enable searching by employers and recruiters;
- joining a local Toastmaster's group, or similar business network; and
- warm calling – rather than cold calling at random, involves calling targeted employers, based on a referral from someone.

Employ all the hidden job market strategies you can, but ensure the first one is to improve your employability: your career identity; your personal adaptability; and your human and social capital. That way, when the hidden door creaks open, the employer will discover the Phantom, not Fantasyman.

The midway point – the Employee Referral Program

There's a midway point between formal recruiting, and the hidden job market. Some large companies operate an Employee Referral Program (ERP) with a bonus for existing staff to find new employees who ... can do, will do, and will fit.

Some firms offer up to $3000 to encourage their staff to refer people they meet to the HR department for assessment for one or more roles in the business. The process could start with an informal chat at a networking event, and become more formal further down the track. Naturally, you will still need a targeted resume, and you should start developing a one-page pitch. This honours the firm, and honours the person who is helping you. It also shows you're really serious about the job (will do!) and are not just coasting along on your luck.

The advantage to the firm is that they get a constant stream of suitable people to assess, and the staff bonus is far less than a recruiter fee. One of the BIG4 spends $ 1 000 000 a year on their ERP, but believes it saves $ 6 000 000 in recruiting costs!

As well as the ERP bonus, your new champion will also develop the reputation of someone out there working for the firm, and directing valuable assets to it. This increases that person's employability. The story of Roberto in Chapter 1 is probably an example of a middle manager, inspired by the firm's ERP, recruiting a potential employee.

The advantage to you is getting an introduction to the hiring personnel of a firm you already know a lot about. You may encounter a bit of pressure from your friend to take any position offered, so you need to be sure you really want the job, and you're not just coasting along on your luck.

Your Linkedin profile

Getting your Linkedin profile out of the shadows is harder than you'd think.

While recruiters and HR personnel certainly use SEO to identify job candidates, there is little reliable statistical data on how effective these efforts are in filling specific vacancies. We all look good on paper, but may be less attractive to a recruiter on the phone, or in person. Recruiters would have to contact many potential candidates to find the few hopefuls wanting job change. This 'digital cold-calling' may have little result. It's more efficient to advertise jobs, and devote precious recruiter time to sourcing employer vacancies.

Another networking exercise is to 'reach out' to your Linkedin contacts to help your job search. You will be disappointed. One of my clients approached twenty online contacts to arrange informational interviews. Eighteen gave no response, and the two who replied were wary about spending their valuable time on someone they didn't actually know. Your Linkedin contacts aren't your friends.

Despite the disappointing job result stats, you still need a brilliant Linkedin profile so people you meet can investigate you quickly. Unless you're a published author, media spokesperson, or have achieved notoriety with an amusing cat video, you probably won't come up on Google, but you must come up properly on Linkedin. In the ideal world, your resume and Linkedin profile should be congruent. While you can easily tailor your resume to different job applications, the Linkedin profile is less flexible. Yes, you can alter it within seconds, but it's hard to tailor it for the range of different jobs you may be applying for at the same time. These may be different roles in different sectors, so your profile will have to be more general than your tailored resume.

On Linkedin, you can be more engaging with the readers, and allow more of your personality to emerge. I'm always disappointed when I find a profile with a photograph, a job title, and nothing else. It's an opportunity lost.

A great Australian Linkedin resource is the book *120 ways to achieve your purpose with Linkedin* by Sue Ellson, a Melbourne career coach. Her book is comprehensive, and has the detail not possible here.

If you go to career expos, job fairs, industry conferences or professional development activities, you need something to direct people to your Linkedin profile – your networking card.

Your networking card – don't leave home without it!

Ships at sea fly a flag, and passenger aircraft emit a radio signal to identify their civilian status. Your networking card is your flag.

Your flag tells people where you're going. It's like a standard business card but with your areas of expertise and specific skills of interest to a potential employer on the back. List your Linkedin URL, so people can check your skills and qualifications. Keep the card simple – black and white, and no fancy graphics. Don't have 500 cards sitting proudly on your desk – get them out into your 'market', working for you.

Dune Blunberbuss B.Sc. Dip. Dep. **Depellisation Consultant** 📞 0440 111 222 ✉ Dunblun83@gmail.com ⊕ Linkedin URL	PMP certified Logistics experienced Crellel synthesis Registered trainer Australian PR Chinese language

The billboard on the back

Most cards are blank on the back. Yours should be a mini-billboard with a few keywords so the person knows what professional skills you're offering. These will be general, but should spark interest so the person checks your Linkedin profile. A QR code may be self-defeating. It's better for the person to see the information immediately rather than having to jump another hurdle.

Take your cards everywhere. You never know who you'll meet, as one of my young clients, we'll call Ganesh, discovered:

Ganesh had recently arrived in Melbourne and had completed my Matrix Method job search program. He was starting to get interviews, and had booked into the Interview Skills Program with me.

He'd recently attended an assessment centre morning for a casual job in a call centre, and realised he needed to improve his interview presentation.

I asked him about the other people there. There was 'one Aussie guy', and a number of people recently arrived, including a young woman from Canada. Ganesh said he found the assessment activities enlightening, and that he pushed himself to be more outspoken. During the lunch break, the young Canadian woman, turned to him and said; 'The Easter break's coming up ... it's so long ... and I don't have anything to do'. I asked Ganesh if he realised she was suggesting he ask her out. He did understand that, but said he didn't follow through.

I asked him if he gave her his networking card to keep the ball rolling, but because he was already coming for an interview, he didn't bring any cards with him that day. I repeated the 'Don't leave Home without it' line. The good news is that Ganesh never left home without it again, and that within a month got a great first job in his sector doing what he liked doing with a firm that valued him highly.

I hope Ms Canada started carrying her networking cards.

Skilltask 15: Your networking card

Design your networking card with six phrases on the back that give an employer a quick snapshot of you and your capabilities. Include any skills that set you apart from other applicants.

Using the card – your elevator pitch

You get into the elevator to go to floor 25, and suddenly Richard Branson (or some key figure in your industry) calls out: 'Hold that lift!' and you're alone with a major guru for 30 seconds. 'Oh ... good heavens ... I errrr ... I thought you ... oh ... Here's my floor ... that was quick ... bye Sir Richard'. Try this instead:

Name	I read your Linkedin post on leadership last week. My name's Dune Blunderbuss. I wonder if you have a card with you. Here's mine.
Who you are	I'm just completing some research on the depellisation industry because I'm investigating new employment there, and need to find out more about the industry.
What you do and what makes you good at it	I've recently managed a depellisation plant and changed how we coordinated the supply chain and logistics processes – with a good result all round. *(Ensure you pause to let the person respond before you try your call to action!)*
Call to action	I know you've made similar changes in your own area. I wonder if I could call you during the week for a brief chat on the challenges you faced and how you dealt with them.

Now you've seen an example, think about your own situation and develop your own elevator pitch. It sounds 'pushy', but you're worth it.

elevator pitch

ERP

networking card

return of the phantom

job search strategies

job applications

hidden job market

recruiters

LinkedIn

gig economy

job fairs

career expos

Skilltask 16: Elevate yourself

You're attending a networking event or conference this week. Research who will also be attending and fill in the grid below with your ptich.

Name	I recognise you from …
Who you are	I'm just completing …
What you do and what makes you good at it	I've recently …
Call to action	I know you've made …

I think you could develop an elevator pitch, but you don't need a networking card, and you certainly don't need a Linkedin profile. There's a lot of push for everyone on the planet to sign up, but unless you have a professional role, it's just playing around.

A reason regularly offered is that you can connect with university students to check out the courses you're interested in, and receive mentoring to help you make an informed course choice. This sounds good, but well-meaning students won't have any training in mentoring, and could overly influence your decision. Qualified career counsellors are better for this. University students may not be so interested in connecting with school students, and may not follow through properly. Also, they could be as confused as you!

Save Linkedin for final year university.

Maybe the elevator is a Linkedin fantasy. The same scenario could just as well take place at a conference where you're beside the presenter in the coffee queue, or a booth at a job fair. Quite senior people attend industry expos or job fairs to rally the troops. They'll be at the booth talking with participants. Get your networking card working. It's hard to refuse a card, and it opens up a conversation with a professional tone. It's good to demonstrate some link to the person or the company. If you've looked at the conference brochure or the participant list you'll know who is likely to attend. You can also use this strategy at networking events.

Everyone should be ready with a standard elevator pitch, but listening to a dozen in one evening may be tiresome for the besieged industry celebrity. Another way is to turn the attention away from you, and onto the other person. How about saying, 'My name's Dune and I've seen you at these events before. What's your particular interest in this one tonight?' This shows you're interested in the other person. You can give your networking card and your radical views on depellisation at the appropriate moment.

You're interested in others ... now be helpful and offer them something for free. 'Thanks for your card. I've got a short video on depellisation logistics I developed for one of our training sessions. Can I send it to your email during the week?' You'll be remembered because of your helpful nature ... and your insightful views on depellisation logistics!

When networking, you're not asking for a job – don't even mention it.

The ultimate leap – the gig economy

You may decide to bypass conventional employment by diving into the gig economy as a consultant, to pursue short-term contracts. All the practical strategies mentioned in this chapter will be useful in establishing and maintaining this challenging role.

Employers like the flexibility of hiring a contractor on a short-term basis, or an hourly rate. This also could be convenient for you, if you can deal with the uncertainty. One Australian website that puts these gigs together is www.freelancer.com. It lists up to 45 000 jobs, across the world, at various rates. Freelancers bid for the roles listed to determine the contract fee. For example, construction and engineering listings range from $20 an hour to $547 an hour, depending on the role. The site controls the process, thus giving certainly to the arrangements entered into by both sides.

Like any other role, your success here will depend on your employability – your career identity, your personal adaptability, and your human and social capital.

Implementing the strategies in this chapter will see you ahead of other candidates in the recruiting race. In the next chapter, you'll see how recruitment has changed over recent years, and how you 'sell into' this challenging environment.

CHAPTER 12

The 3Rs of recruiting – recruiters, robots, and rorts

Career keywords: contemporary recruiting; intuition and rationality; rise of the robots: recruiter perspective; different recruiter types & executive agents; common recruiting rorts

In the film *Her*, the Joaquin Phoenix character, a divorcing nice guy working in the orange-tinted LA of the near future, starts 'dating' an operations system on his mobile. For a small monthly fee, his deepest emotional needs are sympathetically handled by this perceptive, honey-voiced 'OS' – Her. Things begin well, but deteriorate when she wants her own life, and starts hanging out with another OS who's the custodian of the life work of a dead author. Looks like a robotic relationship is as unpredictable as a human one! Joaquin's sensitive acting humanises this whacky situation. While I hope we never get to this in our personal lives – with recruiting, we're already here.

Recruiter intuition vs robotic rationality

Recruiting, like most human interchanges, is a combination of intuition and rationality. This magic mix isn't always clear to the job applicant, but I can detect it immediately in job ads. The growing trend away from extensive selection criteria responses towards the one-page pitch indicates the triumph of intuition over rationality. However, the growing reliance on robotic processes indicates the resurgence of rationality over intuition. These opposites have always coexisted, and continue to coexist in contemporary recruiting. Your job application needs to push both sets of buttons.

Recruiting changes

Contemporary recruiting is changing fast, mostly due to technology. Many of the repetitive tasks of recruiting are now handled by computer programs that never tire of tedious detail, and have no emotions when sending out thousands of rejection emails – recruiter robots!

Recruiters use robotic systems extensively so they can focus time on their key tasks, and relieve their job pressures. When you understand these pressures you'll understand why there are so many questionable practices in recruiting, and know how to 'sell into' the needs of recruiters. You may have the expectation that recruiters are providing a service to you, and it's they who should be working hard to understand your needs and pressures, but you'll have to play the game with recruiters if you want to develop relationships with them. I recommend you include recruiters in your job search strategies, but don't become reliant on them. To orient you to recruiting, we'll explore the rise of the robots, understand the roles of various recruiters, and then find explanations for some of the unsatisfactory recruiting procedures you will encounter.

Rise of the robots

First we had the paperless office. Now we have the personless office! If you get insurance, do banking, and buy products online, you may never relate to a real person, but do everything through robotic systems, and recorded messages. We're now at a cusp in recruiting history when most of the recruiting activities can be carried out using similar robotic systems – personless recruiting!

ATS software can parse and rank resumes, and generate the interview list. With developments in voice recognition software, the final piece of the robotic plan for world domination is in place – assessing interviews with voice recognition software like Dragon Professional to identify 'people of interest'. If ATS can recognise keywords and the block of meaning surrounding them within a written sentence, then analysing voice recognition software to do the same with a spoken sentence is barely more difficult. Transcription from voice to writing is 98% accurate! The recruiting process could be set up by a recruiter, handled by software, with the final decision made by the coordinating human. There is high pressure on recruiters and HR managers to use this process. This liberates recruiters to spend more time contacting employers to source the jobs that give them their power.

There'll be a barrage of opposition to these statements – 'it's impractical, it's degrading, it's inhuman, it's immoral, it's unfair!' Apart from 'impractical' – I agree totally! Our opinions will count for nothing, because there's a huge economic incentive for recruiting to deploy this. Recruiters are just as human as we are, and we all want quick, easy, and cheap solutions to our problems. Those without a blender amongst ye, throw the first electric fry-pan!

The frequent robotic tool used by recruiters is the ATS, mentioned in Chapter 9. It's used to improve work efficiency in processing the avalanche of applications from all over the world for that one advertised position. Anyone, anywhere, can check Australian online job boards and submit a speculative application. These applications clog the system, and ATS unclogs it.

Recruiters don't tell you they're using an ATS product – and they certainly won't tell you which one. There are over twenty systems, like Taleo, being marketed in Australia. These range from the old and simple to the sophisticated and expensive.

These robotic systems:

- review electronic applications;
- reject unsatisfactory resumes;
- send rejection emails;
- parse the content of the successful resumes;
- place the parsed resume content in a database for interrogation by the recruiter;

- schedule telephone interviews; and
- summon the top applicants for an interview with the recruiter.

The recruiter has no reason to see your resume until these automatic and instantaneous operations are completed. Most resumes will not be seen by a human reader. It looks like the Olympic hurdles, and you could fall at any stage, but let it not be hurdle one.

This approach may sound insane, because it rejects good applicants. If the system identifies only one in a hundred applicants as suitable, those few will be enough to enable a hiring decision. Traditionally, only about six in a hundred applications would be suitable anyway!

If this is unfair, your only satisfaction will be in defeating the robots, and this can be done – Dr Who defeats them every week. With the job application strategies presented in this book you can turn robots into allies, by understanding them, and feeding them an enticing diet of the career information they crave.

The recruiter mantra

When assessing candidates the recruiter has the same hiring mantra as the employer:

- Can the person do the job?
- Will the person do the job?
- Will the person fit in?

The recruiter has been hired by the employer to fill specific vacancies, and so, is a delegate of the employer. The first loyalty is to the employer who is paying the bill. The recruiter has no obligation to get you a job, or give you any advice. This explains why you're just a pawn in the recruiting exercise, and why you're treated so badly. I'm not excusing it – just explaining it.

Dealing with recruiters

If you're qualified and experienced (and understand ATS) you'll be in demand by recruiters. They'll see you like washing powder on the supermarket shelf – something to be sold as quickly as possible, to get the next pack on the rack.

 If you see a suitable position advertised on the recruiter website and call, you'll be screened to see if you warrant being connected. The recruiter will have a brief chat and request your resume – that means now. If you get a call back within ten minutes, you're a hot property. If it's after 5.00 pm, you're warm. If you don't get a call by six, you'll never get one. Your desperate calls won't be returned, and your pleading emails won't be read. If the recruiter can't sell you immediately, there'll be no helpful feedback on your niggling faults – you just don't have three-way washing action with dynamic fabric elasticity delivering perfect enwhitenment. You won't get calls back from recruiters until you improve the formula.

When it gets to interviews, Ben always gets them because he lists 'Actor – Part-time, Nextdoor. The employers won't give you a job just for that, but they're sucked in by something different on the resume. The interviewers aren't that interested in his role as Rozzer, but the guys always have questions about Sasha Stardust, and the older ones try to get an autograph from Grit for their daughters. The girls really like a 'bad boy'!

Actually, the true Grit is a real law-abiding citizen. He's older than he looks and has finished a Chinese language course at uni. He's even been in the army reserve for three years.

Now that Ben's doing his final year in bio-science, he's applying for some internships before he and the girlfriend go to Brazil for the exchange year. Word came through, and he got the exchange. He'll have to ditch the Rozzer role for a bit, and the writers say they could have him and Grit disappear mysteriously, and then get written back in after Brazil. They could even disappear in Brazil, with some dodgy Grit stuff. The career counsellor says that Ben's 'career identity' is moving on. It sure is. Funny how he's doing the same course as the girlfriend (it's different unis, as she got a really high entrance score and went to 'The' university. The subjects are the same – even the same textbooks). There's nothing weird about it. They're just interested in the same things – it's not some big romance.

Think of something you do that makes you look different, and put it on your resume. It could be some sports team, or a volunteer organisation where you help others. This will be a practical demonstration of your core skills, and shows that you're connected to the community. Call that section of your resume Community and Volunteer (not Interests) and show the skills you developed with the activities.

Practise writing it here.

Recruiters must fill a job properly, and not just hammer a round peg into a square hole. They usually don't get their full fee until the candidate has been in the position for three months. At that time, you'll have a formal meeting with your manager to review your job description, and performance. This is a two-way conversation and you may make suggestions to improve your role in the unit, and discuss any new duties. There should be a discussion on salary and conditions. It's generally accepted that if either side wants to separate at this point, there are no hard feelings. The only hard feelings will be the recruiter's.

Dos and don'ts

You should list with several recruiters, but inform each one. Ethical recruiters tell you to list with up to three recruiters to cover more territory. Recruiters sometimes work together, and split the fee. If you list with a lot, and you're a good candidate, you may get several recruiters sending your resume to the same employer, as they try to cut in on the territory of their competition. Overlisting looks desperate.

If a recruiter has advertised a job, never contact the employer directly. This bypass move is recommended in Linkedin posts promoting 'hidden job market' strategies, but a recruiter position is not a 'hidden job market' entity. It's a position that has been allocated to a recruiter to fill, and is advertised on the recruiter website, and promoted actively to appropriate candidates. Ethical employers won't like your attempt to subvert the system they're paying for. They've hired the recruiter to do a job, and expect to pay the agreed fee for a suitable result. This breach of trust will probably terminate your relationship with the recruiter.

There are plenty of questionable recruiting practices detailed in upcoming paragraphs, but there's no reason for you to adopt deceptive behaviour. Employers want honest and congruent people, so demonstrate those qualities with your behaviour throughout the recruiting process.

Sometimes you see Linkedin posts giving cute advice on dealing with recruiters, ranging from sitting in reception all morning hoping to ambush your victim, to delaying your calls back. These strategies are ineffective, and waste the time you could use productively. Reception will alert the recruiter to use the back door. If you try a tease by delaying contact, you'll be dropped for a more compliant candidate. In playing recruiter games, you're an amateur!

Types of recruiters

HR recruiters

Large organisations have an HR department that recruits staff. They play by the rules, but may contract private recruiters to do the job for them.

Executive agents

Executive agents, employment consultants or people with similar titles are different from recruiters. With these, the job applicant is the client, paying the executive agent to secure a job. Executive agents don't have any jobs to dispense. They use all the methods you use ... search job boards, check vacancies on company websites etc. They also say they use 'employer networks' but it's difficult to assess what these could be. The employer doesn't pay any fee, and may be attracted by filling a vacancy for free. That's the competitive advantage the executive agent has over recruiters. The recruiters' competitive advantage is having real jobs to start with. Most executive agent time is spent convincing potential job applicants to sign up, and pay up!

If recruiters fill 7% of Australian positions, the success rate of executive agents would be minuscule.

It's a business decision for the individual to source a recruiter, or hire an executive agent to search for a job. If you pay the agent from the first salary gained it could be a good deal. No money should be paid up front, as there's no way to guarantee that anything else happens. Agents put on pressure to get money in advance, with fees up to $2000. There's no government regulation of this – it's just an agreement between the two people.

My advice on dealing with executive agents – buyer beware!

HR hybrids

There are a number of small firms offering everything – HR, recruiting, career advice, resume writing, and executive agent operations. They provide HR functions from payroll to policy for other small firms that can't afford their own HR professionals. These 'HR Hybrids' may undertake recruiting for these other small firms.

On the other side of the table, they offer career advice, and write resumes and job applications (for a fee) for job seekers. They may also charge fees to job seekers to find them a job, and so operate as executive agents. So, they could derive a fee from the employer to recruit staff, charge job seekers a fee to write the resume, and also demand a fee to give access to the jobs they're recruiting for. They may then do the interviewing for that job, and recommend one of their own job seekers. If the fees are transparent, you can make a business decision about working with these firms, but multiple fees for the same service fester conflicts of interest. Conflict of interest means conflict of loyalties and conflict of values, with a focus on fees from the candidate, not contribution of value to the candidate.

E-recruitment

Recruiters traditionally advertised their vacancies on job boards, their own websites, and in newspapers. The digital world expands their options.

With millions of professional profiles listed on platforms like Linkedin, recruiters can undertake targeted searches for potential candidates and follow up with personal calls hoping to spark the interest of people they can place. Despite the hype, there is scant evidence of the number of jobs filled by this method. However, you need to ensure that your profile listed on the various platforms is able to be searched and retrieved by these assertive recruiters. Set up your profile using SEO principles. Your Linkedin headline is a key resource, so don't waste the space with 'Chief Managing Magician' or 'Super Sales Wizard', and certainly not 'Unemployed accountant seeking new opportunities'. No recruiter would ever type those words into the search box, but will try more prosaic titles like 'experienced accountant Sydney'. Link your headline to the position description of the job you want.

Skilltask 17 A Sense of Entitlement

Choose a job title that you know a recruiter will use, and make yourself easy to find.

Job titles of positions you want	Alter your Linkedin headline to suit

Open your own doors

I tell all my professional clients to include recruiters as part of their strategy, but to keep applying independently. Recruiters can open doors for you, but with your own efforts, so can you.

Recruiter rorts and how to avoid them

I tell my recruiter colleagues that recruiters are like naughty puppies. You can bribe and cajole them to do what you'd like them to do, but nothing will happen. Then, they'll suddenly do it – generally at a time most inconvenient for you.

There are many questionable recruiting practices you'll encounter. You can complain, but you won't be able to change this. Like the naughty puppies, they know they can get away with it, because you need a warm and cuddly friend.

Sometimes you'll see a job advertised online that's in your sector, with a prestigious 'national company,' in the perfect location, that seeks your exact qualification and length of experience, and offers the salary you know you deserve. It sounds too good to be true ... and it is. Recruiters will advertise fake jobs to get a batch of resumes they can sift through at a later stage, or to estimate the present strength of labour market supply. If you apply for this advertised Uberjob and ring to enquire on the progress, you'll be told the position has just been filled by an outstanding person – the too-good-to-be-true candidate for the-too-good-to-be-true job.

Employers also suffer deception. I know an IT manager with large national companies who often contracted recruiters to fill management vacancies. Recruiters usually sent six candidates: two were outstanding, and highly desirable; two were fairly good, but had some questions over them; and two were quite unsuitable, and would have struggled in the role. He felt the recruiters were making the point that there were only a few really great candidates out there, but that they'd worked vigorously to get them. I have a parallel explanation. I think that recruiters ration their good candidates, and would never waste six outstanding candidates on one job. If they did, then five candidates would be discouraged. They also like to give their tier-two candidates some experience in real interviews. Tier-three candidates are always complaining that they never get interviews, so they occasionally get tossed a bone for a job they won't get. When I put this to recruiters, they snarl like naughty puppies.

Recruiters can be assertive in sourcing jobs from employers.

I have a friend who is the managing director of a small but profitable insurance brokerage who'd advertised for a Business Development Manager. As soon as his ad was listed, he got a call from a recruiter in another city attesting that they'd found 'the perfect candidate' for the position. My friend told him to pass details on to Mr Perfect, and get him to send in an application. The recruiter obviously wanted to set up a contract with the MD to promote one of his own candidates. This was a recruiter sourcing a job he could later fill from the overflowing filing cabinet of job applicants.

There are also practices in using psychometric assessments that are unethical, but that are used regularly. When doing my Myers-Briggs Type Indicator accreditation course, we were told that using the MBTI as part of recruitment or promotion is unethical. The MBTI is a self-assessment system identifying the person as having one of sixteen personality types. That's all it does, and what you do with this information is up to you and your career coach. It's a form of racism to use the MBTI to compare people in the recruiting process. We don't hire people because of eye colour. We don't refuse to hire short people. We supply a ladder if the job needs it. We shouldn't be hiring for personality type either because people shouldn't have to change their personalities. If a specific job needs a particular human skill, we can train somebody who has the desire, motivation, and qualifications to undertake the role.

It's also impractical to use any personality assessment system to predict success in a specific work role – people will just alter their answers to reflect what they think the role requires. This happened with a colleague of mine who we'll call Jenny.

Jenny had applied for a paramedical position via a specialised recruiter. As well as the interview and reference checks, she was required to take the MBTI, because they seemed to be looking for a particular personality type – as well as a qualified and experienced professional! It wasn't clear if this request had come from the employer, or whether it was the routine of the recruiter. Jenny guessed at the personality characteristics being sought, and answered the questions accordingly – thus giving an incorrect MBTI result. She was naturally allocated to a different personality type from her real one. She did not get this particular position, but it wasn't clear that the 'invented' MBTI type had anything to do with the decision. Not only is it unethical to use the MBTI in the recruitment process ... it's also ineffective, because people may distort their MBTI type to progress in the recruitment process.

You can rage against the rorts, but you can't change them. Nothing will change while the traditional economic bond between employer and recruiter remains in place.

What do you do?

Selling into the recruiter expectations will save your time and energy, as you'll be concentrating on jobs that you have a realistic chance of being offered. But how do you do this?

The first strategy is to select three reputable recruiters, and deal only with them. If you're suddenly contacted by another, by all means assess their suitability, as there may be a genuine job to be filled.

The second strategy is to precisely target each job application to save the recruiter time. It's better to send in two outstanding applications than twenty cut-and-paste concoctions. Don't even think of applying for positions if you're deficient in the qualifications or experience stated. If the ad states 'three years' experience', then eighteen months will not do. If the recruiter tells the employer that nobody has three years, but there's a great candidate with eighteen months, the employer will say to search harder – because that's what the employer's paying for.

The third strategy is to ensure that you set up your resume for ATS software, even though you won't know the exact system being used to filter applications.

The final strategy is to be totally honest with your recruiter. If re-framing is needed – leave it to the professional!

In the recruitment process, there are many players – real and robotic. You now know who they are, and what they want. If you can understand their needs, they can open doors for you, and you'll start to see the results from your hard career work. You now understand recruitment robotic processes, and with the interview, you can get back to dealing with a human.

CHAPTER 13

The job interview part 1: Be prepared

Career keywords: interview = outcome; job applicant to job candidate; interview types; after the interview

During the job application process you've dodged the robotic nanorays, and finally have a real interview with a real person, or a panel of them – your first interview. Congratulations! You've graduated from 'job applicant' to 'job candidate'.

So far, the focus has been on eliminating unsuitable applicants. Now, the aim is to select the most appropriate candidate. If six people are being interviewed, most are capable of doing the job, but each in different ways. Your aim during the interview is to demonstrate how your Unique Value Proposition is the best outcome for the employer.

What's an interview?

You don't have many interviews in your working life, and it's hard to control the expectations of interviewers you've just met. At its best, a job interview should be a professional conversation between equals – an 'inter' 'view'.

There are different types of interviews, and your first task is to figure out which type of interview you'll be undergoing. Here are the main ones:

- screening interview – telephone or video
- group interview
- assessment centre
- panel interview
- individual interview
- case interview
- partner interview
- 'just a chat' interview

They're all different and need different types of preparation. Even a fabulous candidate, fabulously prepared, can be tripped up with an unfamiliar format or unexpected questions.

Screening interview

The telephone or video interview appears the most daunting, but it's only the first hurdle in the interview Olympics. The aim here is to screen out as many people as possible, in the quickest time, at the lowest cost.

Screening interviews may be conducted by a real person, but generally they're your phone responses to a set of questions recorded for later analysis. If selected for this automated telephone torture, you'll get a code for an online service. Log in and listen to each question, and then give your answer. One advantage is that you usually have some opportunity to review your response, and do it again.

This 'analysis' done on your performance may be 30 seconds of disinterested listening by the HR intern until you make a major error, misunderstand the question, or gargle your response after a hasty gulp of water. You could imagine this junior tiring quickly when listening to a hundred poor responses. If your responses are competent, you'll certainly stand out, and get moved through. Now you know your core skills, you can be confident in presenting your case concisely.

The other possibility is that, with improved voice recognition software, a computer robot could analyse your responses, thus cutting out the human element totally. It would be seeking appropriate keywords and the context around them. While this sounds frightening, at least the robot won't doze off after applicant 33. Each response will get the same attention. The robot will never be perfect, but it can identify a satisfactory number of appropriate applicants to push through to the next stage of the selection process.

Action: Practise answering simple behavioural questions highlighting your core skills, and review them before submitting. During the video interview, look directly at the camera on your PC, not at the image on the screen. Wear professional attire, not your best pyjamas – and take down your Beyonce posters.

Use all the time you're given and make it easy for the bored listener to decide to accept you, and eliminate the other gargling applicants. There's no appeal from this – one gargle and you're out! The successful applicants will go through to the next round, which could be the group interview.

Group interview

Group interviews are often group business tasks. In one such activity much favoured by the BIG4 consulting firms, the group was given a series of promotional options for a national business client, and a notional $25 000 budget. Each person had to make recommendations on allocating this budget across three promotional projects: financing a yacht in the Sydney to Hobart Yacht Race; establishing a university travelling scholarship; and sponsoring a school in Timor.

The session started with a fun ice-breaker – everyone stated something they'd done that was unusual. Recorders then took notes on how members put their pitch.

Action: Prepare a short personal introduction for the group. It doesn't have to be brilliantly witty (they're not hiring you for improv) but think of something unique that people will remember – and write down. Keep it light.

Assessment centre

An assessment centre is not a place, but a process incorporating several of the interview modes discussed in this chapter in a round robin of groups to assess the applicants in various settings. It's often used by large companies filling many positions.

Usually, there is an initial presentation on the company and its goals, and a listing of the various roles being offered. There could be up to thirty applicants, split into smaller groups for the various exercises. There could be a written exercise and psychometric testing before moving on to group interviews. There could be a practical teamwork exercise to see how you relate to a group. I once observed a group activity where the six group members were given a stack of newspapers, adhesive tape and scissors, and told to replicate the Sydney Harbour Bridge across a space between two desks. This wasn't assessing engineering prowess, but teamwork skills. All these activities are observed by the recorders in the corner, registering who does what. These notes are later used to identify applicants of interest for follow-up.

There are two types of psychometric assessment – skills testing and personality assessment. There is a correct answer for a test, but not for an assessment. The testing element may include English comprehension, cognitive reasoning and numeracy exercises. Personality assessments attempt to measure your personality characteristics on some type of scale. Just answer these questions truthfully, and don't try to guess the answer you think they're seeking. Your guess may be wrong, and depict a confused person. There may be over 300 statements to read, and you won't be consistent unless you answer truthfully. There are internal checks to expose those gaming the system.

Action: It's hard to prepare for assessment centre activities, but having a good attitude to them is important. While your team members are competitors, be respectful of all, acknowledge their contributions, and remember their names. Speak up in the group activities so the recorders know you're there. Get involved and have fun. It's only part of the selection process. Weight is also given to your resume, academic record, and referee reports.

You can practise on websites like www.shldirect.com . This website has sample tests and explains the correct answers. Completing *The Australian Career Passport* will give you practical experience in dealing with personality assessments.

You'll get assessment centre details in advance. Study the program so you're not rattled by the different group exercises and room changes. Be prepared for a short individual interview during the time.

Panel interview

This is the standard interview method, conducted by a panel of three or more people with different roles in the organisation. There is usually the unit manager, an HR representative, and another person co-opted for the task. This could be a fairly senior person, or someone with technical knowledge of your area of expertise.

Action: When you're contacted, ask for the names and roles of people on your panel. Try to find them on the company website, Google, or Linkedin so you know their backgrounds. They may have done something outstanding you should know about.

Direct your answer mainly to the person who asked the question, but also look at the others to keep them included in the discussion. Check on the person taking the interview notes, which may be recorded on a large tracking sheet. While that person is writing, you're doing well. When the person stops taking down your thoughts, you've probably started waffling. Stop the waffle, and move on to the ice cream, or wash up and wait for the next question.

Take targeted supporting documentation to the interview to leave with the panel. Ideally, you should have prepared the *Interview PowerPack*, which is discussed later in this chapter. If not, then find a flyer for a professional development session you've organised, or a notification for some community group function, as evidence of your community engagement. Refer to it during the interview and have several copies for the panel. I suggest handing copies to the chair of the panel to distribute to other members. People take a document more seriously from an authority than an applicant. It also shows respect for the chair.

At a high professional level, I usually help my clients prepare a 30/60/90 day plan for their prospective position. They find a place to bring it up in the interview and leave copies with the panel. As well as giving relevant information to the panel to make an informed decision, you're also demonstrating your capacity to run a professional meeting. You'll be remembered!

Individual interview

As you advance in the process you may have individual interviews with the different professionals you'll be working with. This is a golden opportunity to find out more about the company, and roles at different levels. You'll know about these interviews in advance, so prepare for each one and think about the questions you would like to ask each of these experienced professionals. Even if they are not the high professionals you would prefer to be talking with, each has history in the organisation you've said you're interested in, and has wisdom gained over time. They're offering to share, so respect that.

Action: Ensure you know your stuff, and understand the organisation you've applied to join. Failing to do this is a key fault that recruiters report in applicants. Whatever you've studied, there's a large body of knowledge you've become expert in. My younger clients forget all this, and start making it up as they go along. Ensure you revise the theory and main models before you start your interviews. You passed exams in this!

Case interview

By this stage they're really serious about you because they've allocated an experienced professional in your field to grill you on your professional knowledge and practical capacity to use it. This person is on your side, and may give you some prompting to 'get it all out'. Of course, this person is on the side of all candidates, because that gets the best information.

In the case interview you're given some information about a business scenario and have to come up with potential solutions to the key business problem posed by the circumstances. Evaluate all options, but give a clear recommendation on action for your solution. There could be lengthy details, and the interviewer will encourage clarifying questions. While this certainly is a 'structured' interview, lateral thinking is encouraged. A case scenario could look like this:

> *One of our clients is Casla, a major electric vehicle manufacturer, now considering Australian development operations for their new 4X4 vehicle – the Elektrak. They are aware of the current flight of car manufacturers out of the country, but are confident of renewed Australian Government interest in car manufacturing with an environmental element. They are confident that the time is right for a high-tech, environmentally favourable, politically acceptable plan for jobs and growth to be put forward to Commonwealth and State Governments.*

> *Casla sees two possible manufacturing options – developing the design and engineering in Australia but manufacturing in China, or undertaking all design, engineering and manufacturing here, using the abandoned car plant sites left by the exiting car manufacturers.*

> *Could you advise Casla on the factors to be considered for both options, and make a recommendation on which option should be favoured?*

There is, of course, no correct answer. The aim is for you to harness your considerable technical business knowledge to engage with the problem.

Action: Remember that you've spent years gaining this kind of knowledge. If you've completed a finance degree, search back into your course to find some suitable business models from your units or business practicum experience. Don't wade into this problem without having made a decision on which business model to use to organise the information. You could start with a SWOT analysis to show you can organise the territory before you begin generating solutions. Think out loud, engage with the interviewer, and ask for clarification as you go along. You can ask for a few minutes to review the situation and draft a plan, but the more you vocalise, the more you'll engage. This person is the professional you aspire to be who has been sent as your guardian angel for the interview. It's not about an answer, but assessing that you can use some recognisable process to develop clear options. Whatever the sector – finance, medicine, engineering – use the theory you have studied to demonstrate your understanding.

With a good recommendation from this guardian angel, you'll get promotion to 'credible candidate'.

Partner interview

The partner interview is daunting, but you will enjoy it. You'll be in the presence of the outstanding professional you aspire to be, and the partner will be highly interested in what you bring to the firm. The partner will know everything about you, and will jolly you into a relaxed state. Suddenly, the time will be up, and you'll be walking on air – full of motivation to be the best whateveritis they've ever hired, and inspired to work 24/7 for the company. It's a win/win!

Action: Find out everything about the partner. The person may be a member of the professional association's national committee, or have written articles and books. Read them, and have some questions or observations on the content to bring up in the interview. This person has done the homework on you. You should 'show some respect', and do the same.

Just a chat

Don't believe a word of it! Prepare for a formal interview, as I found out early in my working life:

A long time ago in a galaxy far away I was an enthusiastic young teacher, and had been offered an International Teaching Fellowship to China. This was just as the country was opening up in the 1980s, and I was very keen to see what was happening. While not quite playing cricket for Australia, it was a great honour to be selected for this international posting.

I'd been through the full selection process, including a panel interview where a panel member asked me in Chinese what my aim was in applying for the fellowship! I'd apparently given a good enough answer, as I was accorded this highly desirable international posting. A couple of days after I'd been informed, I got a call from a senior departmental officer telling me that the Deputy Director, International Programs wanted to see me. The officer assured me that it was just a formality that this senior bureaucrat wanted to give me the tick of approval. I was a little apprehensive at being summoned into head office, not knowing what was expected.

Just as I left the Language Centre that afternoon, I grabbed a few student projects that had just been submitted and slipped them into my bag – just in case the senior bureaucrat wanted some evidence that I was as good a teacher as everybody attested.

To the muted 'ping' of an arriving lift, the secretary ushered me into the office for the grilling. The bureaucrat sat behind an enormous desk – completely clear. The ceiling-high bookshelves were equally empty, save for a leather-bound copy of the Education Act. The bureaucrat picked up the phone to hold all calls! He was a very engaging man, and, of course, pretty sharp. We had a pleasant chat about his International Teaching Fellowship to France in 1962, and how the experience had prepared him to take more responsibility on his return. As we were getting to the end of the banterfest, he said, 'Well, what have you brought in to show me today?' In triumph, I took out my student assignments, and discussed the link between explicit grammar instruction and experiential learning assessment in an integrated curriculum setting. On parting, he said he would be very happy to recommend me for the award.

I learnt two things that day: always be prepared for a formal interview; and maintain a completely clear desk so people know you're fully in control of your job.

Action: Join the scouts or guides when young – and be prepared!

Speaking of which, now that we're familiar with the different types of interviews, let's look at how to be prepared, plus some general tips.

Before the interview

Be as prepared as the interviewer. Prepare a small folio of supporting documents to leave behind. If it's a panel, have enough so each member gets a copy. This *Interview PowerPack* could include:

- a SWOT analysis indicating the main issues for the firm;
- your 30/60/90 day plan for your role;
- supporting flyers for professional activities you've coordinated; and
- abstracts for conference papers you've given, or outlines of relevant assignments you've written.

Don't label your folio *Interview PowerPack*. Something like 'Brixted Company, Graduate Position, Supporting Documents' will suffice.

You know the value you're bringing with your technical skills and core skills, but you must research employers thoroughly. The company website will give you some rosy information. You'll have a shiny company brochure, supplied by HR. There are more objective information sources like the ASIC website for company information, and the major online databases like www.marketLine.com , or www.ibisworld.com . The www.glassdoor.com site gives you a company perspective from the point of view of current staff members – anonymous of course. The advantage of these sites is that they show you the specific issues each company is facing. The financial press will have industry outlook articles, and features on particular companies.

You also need to understand their 'pain point'. This has influenced the decision to hire a new employee, and you need to sell into it. I recall an interview I had with an executive of one of the BIG4 in 2008, as the Global Financial Crisis hit. He said:

> *Over the last few years we've been coordinating the assets of our corporate clients to manage wealth. They've been rolling out targeted expansions, and mergers and acquisitions have been involved in this. Now, we're managing risk, and helping our clients offload unprofitable businesses and business units. They're trying to claw back as much hard cash as they can.*

With this information, I was able to advise my clients to emphasise their business valuations expertise rather than their mergers and acquisitions background. Your employer research will tell you if the business is expanding, contracting, or just treading water. This will alter the skills you emphasise at your interview.

After the interview

As soon as you've left the interview, find a quiet spot and write down every question, and your answers. This will train you in interview technique. Also, you may have misunderstood a major question. You'll be surprised at what you really knew, but omitted to say. I tell my clients immediately to send an email with a clarifying response. In the old days, I would send a fax. I'd have a polite opening thanking the person for the interview and saying that I felt I hadn't given full information on question three, and here was my revised response. With the fax, my response would be on the desk when the person got back after the interviews. With email, you're relying on the person to log in. This doesn't look desperate. You're just clarifying one of your statements.

There's a lot of US internet advice encouraging you to send a hand-written thank-you note to the main interviewer. I think this is an unnecessary Edwardian extravagance that creates confusion. Is the interviewer expected to reply, or send you a holiday postcard from the Bahamas? Are you trying to re-run the interview? Are you looking for a date? Unless you really need to send an explanatory email – leave it, and get on with your life.

Preparation is important for good interview outcomes. Know what type of interview you're facing, and prepare accordingly.

CHAPTER 14

The job interview part 2: Questions and answers

Career keywords: STAR technique; beyond the STARs; your questions; the essential question; three-step strategy

The interview is an integral part of the hiring process, and this is where your personality comes in. People hire people, not a set of disembodied skills. Don't underestimate the strength of the personal element. In the interview, skills and personality come together, and recruiters and employers look for congruency. When you walk into the interview, you must be congruent with your resume and your job application. The easiest way to be congruent is to be honest – so be yourself. You do have to control your behaviour in the interview, but do it within your usual personality. Don't try to become extroverted for your 30-minute interview, if that's not your nature. This book will help you with answering behavioural questions, but any dishonesty or exaggeration will be detected immediately. You might do six interviews in a year – HR professionals do six before lunch!

Now let's get to the heart of interviewing – the questions.

Types of questions

The job interview is about assessing KSAOs and has three question types to do this: information questions; hypothetical questions; and behavioural questions.

Information questions are fairly clear. The interviewer may go through your resume and ask questions about your previous roles to clarify any issues, like major gaps or sudden role changes. The interviewer may also want to assess your level of technical knowledge with questions like: 'What are the elements of a good marketing campaign?'

Hypothetical questions invite you to speculate on how you would solve a specific work problem like: 'How would you select a marketing agency for the new Ladidas Majors range?'

These questions are now less common, and have been replaced with behavioural questions.

The **behavioural** approach is based on the work of industrial psychologist Bill Owens and replaces the unverifiable hypothetical question with one based on real candidate behaviour. The idea is that past behaviour predicts future behaviour. It's an efficient way for you to deliver relevant information to the employer to make an informed hiring decision. Questions could be like: 'Could you tell us about a marketing campaign you devised within a particular budget?', or 'How have you dealt with a new challenge?'

Other questions could sound like this:

- Describe how you ...
- Tell us about a time when ...
- Can you think of a situation where...
- Was there ever a time when ...
- Have you ever encountered ...

The hypothetical gives you the situation, and you respond. With behavioural questions the recruiter lets you define the situation, and talk about what actions you really took. If you follow a simple pattern, they're quite easy to answer. This gives the recruiter real information, and gives you a lot of control. Base your answer on a real situation you remember well, and use the STAR technique to organise your responses.

Be an interview STAR

The STAR technique for interview control should now be well known by recruiters, employers and candidates. Employers like the STAR method because it establishes consistency across interviews, and gives a structure for HR operatives who aren't qualified career counsellors. It provides some hooks for the candidate to hang some impressive facts that may otherwise tumble out in discord. Even a coffee interview with a managing director can progress better with a bit of structure used by the executive candidate.

Linking up the STAR concept with the appropriate language is a powerful tool to get your points across. Let's now look at the technique in detail.

Situation: Briefly describe the situation of your choice. Give just enough information to set the scene for the recruiter. Cut out unnecessary details. This shows your capacity for awareness.

'When I was working as a ... in the ... there was a situation that came up in which ...' and you're away.

Task: Say what you thought the problem or issue was. A lot of the books and websites omit this step. They also are very confused about what 'task' means and there are several explanations that are unconvincing. One is that you should discuss what your usual job duties were. I can't see that doing this adds anything to the technique.

Don't leave this step out as, if there was no issue, why were you taking action? This shows your capacity for analysis.

'When I evaluated the situation I realised that my task was to ...'

Action: Say what action you personally took. There may have been others who helped as well. You can mention that, but concentrate on what you actually did. This shows capacity for judgement and follow-through.

'The action I took was to ... This seemed to be working so I continued to ... and then informed my supervisor' or 'That action didn't seem to be working so I decided to ... instead'.

Result: Say what the result was. 'The result of the action I took was ...' This shows capacity for evaluation.

The result should have been basically successful or at least have improved the situation, but it doesn't have to be 100% successful every time. If it wasn't totally successful, this gives you a chance to show how you would change your actions the next time. Evaluation of actions and changing tack when needed shows flexibility.

You can follow this pattern explicitly and it really helps interviewers if you use the words – **situation, task, action** and **result** in your answers in the appropriate sections. They can see where you are, and will fill out their notes fully. This is a win/win. It makes their job easy, so they can recommend you.

We could reasonably expect behavioural questions to cluster around the ten Core Skills for Work, which are now appearing in the employer lingo.

Talk the talk

Let's test the STAR approach and see how you can use it in your employment situation. There is one general exercise, one exercise for ♟, and another for a wide range of people working in an organisational setting. The system is also useful for senior executives – though the results may be measured in millions. Wherever you work, it's important to think deeply to come up with real examples. If you just Google '199 Knock Out STAR Answers' and try to remember those, you won't know what to say at the first interrogation, and it's your interview that'll be knocked out!

> Much of the info here is beyond what you need for the kinds of part-time jobs you'd be applying for. The ten core skills are still totally relevant to you, but you have to understand them in the real situations you've been in. You've probably been involved in some kind of team – sports team, debating team, chess club, charity fund-

raising, something at youth group, and more. You can find plenty of evidence that you can 'connect and work with others'. You've also probably had a holiday job and related to other staff, a manager, and various customers. You have plenty of examples of your core skills.

Let's take an example of someone with customer service experience who's applying for a new part-time job. Maybe the question is: 'Could you tell us about a time when you showed your initiative to improve something at work, or in your sports team?'

STAR	Sample sentences you could use
Situation: Briefly describe the situation of your choice with just enough information to set the scene.	*When I was working as a grocery assistant at Fruitorama, a small family run business, I noticed a lot of fruit wastage throughout the week.*
Task: Say what you thought the problem or issue was.	*The issue was that customers were reluctant to buy the small pieces of fruit even though they were OK. I thought that presenting them better could be the solution.*
Action: Say what action you took personally.	*The action I took was to separate out all the smaller pieces of fruit early on when they still looked good. I filled small cardboard boxes with a few select items and placed them down low near the checkout stations. I'd noticed we had a lot of young mothers with strollers and thought this would be like the sweets and chocolates at child level in the big supermarkets. The boss thought it was worth a go. I labelled the boxes 'Kids Pack' and priced them at $3.50. It was very successful and the packs were all gone by lunch.*
Result: Say clearly what the result of the action was.	*The result was that we turned a waste product into a 'must have' item. The kids ate more fruit – and so did the mums.*

If you're in high school, or in a TAFE program – you can still be a STAR, but most people interviewing you only want to know that you're honest, reliable, flexible, easy to get on with, and can take direction from supervisors. Now, think of one good example for each of your top core skills, and develop a STAR example for each.

Here's an example for a professional situation. You should try to develop a number of STAR examples using professional work situations. They don't have to be initiatives that changed history, but small, achievable projects that made a difference.

For example you could answer the question. 'Could you tell us about a time when you showed some initiative at work? What did you do and what was the result?'

You could also use it to answer a question like, 'Could you tell me about a time you took responsibility for a project, and what the result was?'

STAR	Sample sentences
Situation: Briefly describe the situation of your choice with just enough information to set the scene.	*When I was working in HR with Oxbiz International a situation came up in which my manager asked me to review the new staff orientation program.*
Task: Say what you thought the problem or issue was.	*The issue was that new staff still made HR enquiries about basic procedures like sick leave rights and superannuation. To answer their questions we generally referred to the same information pack that had been used in orientation and we'd assumed they had understood all of this. However, some information was out of date or slightly inaccurate.*
Action: Say what action you took personally.	*The action I took was to review the full information pack. There were a lot of gaps as it had been put together over the years by different people at different times.* *I also talked to some recent staff and asked them to show me the most useful parts of the orientation pack to indicate what could stay.* *I recommended to my supervisor that the intern assemble an up-to-date pack and include consistent documentation on recent company policies.*
Result: Say clearly what the result of the action was.	*The result was that new staff had a better orientation program. A formal evaluation we did later showed this, and there were fewer enquiries to HR on standard issues.*

Skilltask 18: Follow your STAR

Now apply the technique to your real-life situation. Consider the question *'Could you tell us about a time when you showed some initiative at work? What did you do and what was the result?'* use the STAR approach with some appropriate sentences.

STAR	Sample sentences you could use
Situation: Briefly describe the situation of your choice with just enough information to set the scene.	*When I was working as a ...*
Task: Say what you thought the problem or issue was.	*The issue was that ....*
Action: Say what action you took personally.	*The action I took was ...*
Result: Say clearly what the result of the action was.	*The result was that ...*

STAR challenges

A technical criticism of behavioural interviewing is that it forces you to consolidate your answers around your previous work experience, not around demonstrating the competencies required for the new position.

Always link your STAR example back to the skill that the question is probing.

There is also anecdotal evidence of interview disaster when candidates lift a couple of examples off the internet. One story that may be more than an urban myth is of three MBA candidates for the same position having the identical internet stories of fundraising initiatives which they confidently delivered to an increasingly sceptical panel. An experienced interview panel would not be disconcerted by the pantomime, and would dig deeper with in-depth questioning to confirm authenticity.

Audience ... Ben has an audience of half a million every night as Rozzer! It hit almost a million the night Grit and him stole the underwear from Mrs Crosby's back yard. It was Grit's idea. It was really funny the way they made a catapult with that big one, and ... you know the rest. When they got caught, the way the bullying at home came out in court was really 'poignant' – that's what the media reviews said. It turned the light on why some kids go off the rails. This wasn't just an accident, because the writers had been approached to write that in to draw attention to in-home bullying. It almost got Ben a Logie that year, but it went to Sasha because she was the doctor who told the police her suspicions. Ben was really happy for her.

That was one audience for Ben – unfortunately when he was playing a total idiot! This was a bit of an issue when he had to do the presentation for the Amazon exchange, as that was totally serious.

He got some help from the Career Centre at uni, because he had to do an interview, and a presentation on his goals for the exchange.

The advisor said the interview panel might think he was a privileged young brat with a sense of entitlement used to swanning about on the red carpet, so he had to be really professional and show how his acting job contributed to his maturity to take the exchange. The interview panel is really an 'audience' and that's what they'd be interested in to make the decision.

He also got him to use the STAR approach for his interview questions. One question was: 'Could you tell the panel about any activity you've undertaken that has contributed positively to your community?' Ben used the STAR technique to show how his TV role as an annoying total idiot had helped the whole community come to understand in-home bullying, and know the practical strategies they could use to help reduce it. He knew he'd got it when the chair thanked him for 'turning celebrity into responsibility'.

He did get it, and he's going soon. When he appeared on the red carpet with Sasha Stardust at the Logies that seemed to end it all with the girlfriend. She over-reacted a bit. It was really just an acting gig. With Sasha, it's a professional mentoring relationship – it's not some big romance.

If you were asked in an interview about how you had helped your community, what would you say?

In-depth questioning

Interview panels are improving in assessing candidate authenticity. It could be disheartening for credible candidates who have done the hard preparation to find their neatly packaged STARs being closely grilled by savvy interviewers.

One technique the employer could use to build on the STAR interview information would be drilling down into the candidate's examples. with questions like: 'What did that experience teach you?', 'What did your manager think of how you handled the issue, and what methods did you use to explain it?' You need to go the extra mile here, and be prepared to give precise details of discussions with people around you about the issue in question. It's like a court case – if the defendant leads some key evidence, the prosecution has the right to question it.

These drill-down questions have a hypothetical element to them. If you can 'Crack the Code' in your written job application, you'll be able to do the same in the interview.

Here are some examples of drill-down questions and the core skill they're examining.

Core skill	Behavioural questions	Possible drill down questions
Create and innovate	*Could you tell us about a time when you demonstrated initiative?*	*From your earlier SWOT analysis of our company, could you focus in on one element that you feel could be changed and outline how you would go about that in your role as ……?*
Work with roles, rights, and protocols	*Could you tell us about a time when you changed some work procedures either for yourself or for a work team or unit?*	*If you were implementing the type of change you've talked about, how would you go about estimating the time it would take to register lasting change?*
Identify and solve problems	*How have you evaluated changes in work procedures?*	*What do you think would be a realistic success test for that change?*

The table above shows how drill-down can follow behavioural questions. Questions in the last column seem hypothetical, but they invite you to draw on real career experiences. Each question builds on the previous, and enables the interviewer to drill down into your real experience. In the first question based on an earlier SWOT analysis, you could demonstrate initiative by showing that the job and company have been thoroughly researched for a key business issue, and then use STAR to demonstrate an earlier success in a similar area. Applicants without the relevant experience will struggle with these questions, but not you.

Dealing with the drill-down interrogation needs a good understanding of the company or organisation and its strategic goals. This is an area where even the most competent candidates often stumble. I once had a Master of Accounting student say to me, 'Why do I have to know anything about the company? I'm just an accountant!' My response was, 'So, you want a highly paid position with great career prospects at the heart of company knowledge, but you don't care about the employer, the company, or their clients!'

You must use all means to discover the real needs of the employer to sell into during the interview. This includes uncovering the hidden selection criteria. Even if you're never asked one of these drill-down questions, just thinking about them will produce a better interview.

Your interview is all about authenticity, so uncovering authentic examples of your core skills in action is essential. You also need to keep pace with industry changes, and recruitment developments, to 'boldly go' beyond the STARs, and be able to confront alien questions from distant worlds that will try to disrupt your cosmic answers.

Dealing with difficult questions

Not everybody has a 'standard' life – addiction, bankruptcy, children, diabetes, emergencies, foolhardiness, gin, hedonism, and all the other letters of the alphabet can de-rail your life beyond your control, and affect your employability.

Uncompleted courses may be mentioned, but ensure you state the relevant subjects completed, and what you learnt from the experience. If you list several unfinished courses, you may look like someone who fails to complete things. Don't mention uncompleted courses unless the interviewer does.

Gaps in employment are sometimes an employer concern. If you've been travelling internationally, you may find it difficult to settle into a stable job. Maybe you had a severe health issue that could recur. Maybe you were in prison. With a gap beyond a few months, you can see how an employer's mind could go wild – until you calm it with an honest explanation.

The significance of the resume time gap is sometimes exaggerated. Jim Bright, the author of *Resumes that get short-listed* did some research on this gap. He sent recruiters resumes with clear and substantial gaps, but found that half the recruiters didn't notice them. Those who did were happy with the rest of the resume, and said they'd investigate the gap in the interview. Well – it's now the interview, so how will you handle the difficult questions?

Don't brush aside an intrusive question, but give an answer that is true, understandable, convincing, and that closes down any further enquiry. This is not dishonest or manipulative. It's balancing your privacy with the employer's need to know. If an employer knows there is a gap, and decides to interview you despite this, you're ahead. The employer wants a rational answer to confirm the intuitive feeling, and the 3-step strategy does this.

Skilltask 19: The 3-Step Strategy

Sometimes employers will have a specific concern about employing you and need reassurance before making the offer. You must always be prepared for these concerns and deal with them immediately and effectively. The employer has chosen to interview you, indicating that if the concern can be removed then an offer is possible. Reassurance is needed and you must base this on evidence from your career so far.

The 3-Step Strategy empowers you to deal with the issue clearly. The steps are:

1. Acknowledge the concern
2. Reassure that it will not be a barrier
3. Counteract the idea by offering clear evidence

You could phrase your response like this:
I understand your concern, but let me assure you that it will not be a problem because ...

Concern	Response
I am concerned that coming in from your own start-up business you may find it difficult to fit into a large organisation.	I understand your concern, but let me assure you that it will not be a problem because ...
I am concerned that being highly qualified and experienced in a trade you may find it difficult to take instruction from a younger person.	I understand your concern, but let me assure you that it will not be a problem because ...
I am concerned that ...	I understand your concern, but let me assure you that it will not be a problem because ...

This strategy may not be successful with career gaps due to unauthorised share trading that collapsed the bank, or acts of High Treason. You may have to own your past, and demonstrate you've implemented successful strategies that helped you move up to contributing to society, and its businesses. Choose your referees to attest to this improvement. People turn their lives around every day – I hope you're one of them.

Your questions

If you have no questions at the end of the interview, it will come across as if you're no longer interested in the position, or haven't researched the role.

Be careful about the questions you ask. Salary and benefits questions should never be asked here. Don't ask about anything that was covered in the interview, anything that is commercial-in-confidence, or that the interviewer would be unlikely to know. Don't make the interviewer feel uncomfortable, or have to take a wild guess. Anything that begs a platitude back is also useless. A question like: 'How would you describe the work culture here?' will hardly get the answer: 'It's a cowed organisation controlled by a crazed megalomaniac'. Another question for your potential manager I saw advocated on a Linkedin post was: 'What's the biggest mistake you've ever made here, and what did you learn from it?' The answer may be: 'I once hired an upstart with no judgement, and I learnt never to make that mistake again!' If you've made a bad impression in the interview, you won't turn that around in the last two minutes. If you've made a good impression, don't look like a Smart Alec, or Smart Alecia, now.

Questions could be:

What would be your main expectations of the person in this role over the first couple of months?

Where did the last person in the role move on to?

Could you tell me what the next step in the process is?

The Final Question

Most people say it takes some courage to ask this final question. It certainly puts interviewers on the spot, but experienced people can handle it.

At anything from junior management to top executive positions, most interviewers will expect it, and will be disappointed if you don't ask it.

When you've asked a couple of your lead-in questions, you ask: 'Are there any considerations that you would have that would prevent your offering me the position?' The interviewer should answer you honestly, and that will alert you to any real concerns. If there is a concern, then immediately contest that concern with the 3-Step Strategy – then leave it.

You may have a number of interviews before you get an offer you want. It's a pyramid – a base number of applications, fewer interviews, and even fewer offers at the top. It's easy to get discouraged if the interviews come, but the offers don't. This is, however, a good sign that several employers consider you a credible candidate – and very soon you'll be the right person, at the right time, at the top of the pyramid. When you are, you'll have the happy task of considering your offers, and the challenge of negotiating your result.

CHAPTER 15

Negotiate the numbers

Career keywords: context & risk management; value before valuing; know the market; open options & keep flexibility

Congratulations, you've landed the job. Now you can sit back and relax. Or can you? There's one very important matter yet to be decided – the remuneration package. This is yet another area where you need to be savvy, and apply the new knowledge you've gained by reading this book.

Negotiation takes place in a context, and is about managing risk. If you understand these two things, you'll be able to negotiate constructively in this floating world of cloud and fog.

Understanding the context

All organisations peg specific salary packages to specific positions – the more complex the job, the higher the package. These points can change over time as new jobs replace old jobs. A job is just a cluster of duties determined by some authority. It could be the business owner, the Managing Director, or HR staff. Government or public organisation jobs are clearly defined, and aligned with an easily discovered benefits package. Private businesses often generate a hazy fog you need to penetrate. Their context is about company profits, strategic prioritisation of key business units, and key jobs in those units. Key jobs bringing in a lot of profit are highly paid. This is the context you need to understand in your negotiations. Link your performance and outcomes to the key income stream of the company so you increase your chance of turning on a bigger tap. No employer will increase your salary because you need more money.

Another aspect of context is time. Just after you've been offered the job is a good time to negotiate, because you'll have a good bargaining position. They've just eliminated a lot of people, and know you're the best available. They don't want to crawl back to number two, who may have accepted another offer already.

Another time aspect is your age and seniority. For a graduate position, you don't have much bargaining power. Every year, one of the BIG4 fills 550 internships and 550 graduate positions after an exhaustive selection process involving 22 000 applicants. They get the best 1100 young people, but there's not much difference between number 1100 and number 1101. They really want you, but if your salary expectations are extreme, then going to applicant 1101 is no big deal for them. You need them more than they need you. My advice would be not to try to negotiate a salary increase at the graduate position entry stage. You'll be arguing over a fairly small amount, and this will easily be made up with your first scheduled salary increase. Raise a raise at your performance review, when you've shown what you can do. This is an expected part of the process and shows you can tie your salary package expectations to your outcomes.

If you're a senior appointment with a good track record of increasing value for previous employers, then you have strong bargaining power when hired. You're in a different context because there aren't 21 999 people similar to you, waiting in line. They need you more than you need them.

How to negotiate

Negotiating your benefits can be stressful, but some basic guidelines will help:

- be prepared to *demonstrate* your value before you *state* your value;
- be fully informed on the appropriate packages for similar roles in your industry;
- keep options open for as long as possible; and

- be flexible within the benefit parameters.

Put value before valuing

Demonstrating your value before making a value demand on your benefits package is your key negotiating strategy. Your ability to present your Unique Value Proposition has resulted in the offer, so keep all negotiation focused on value. This value is what you bring, not what you have.

Ben's friends have been getting emails from his Amazon exchange. The girlfriend didn't go, but she got a Rotary to Vermont, so she's pretty happy. She's put it on her CV already! She wanted some time apart. Anyway, they're just friends – it's not some big romance.

Here's part of Ben's email:

'... ha ha. Yes, it's all nuts here! The research post is on a quiet cove and we get into the water to tag them. Yeah – real Steve Irwin! It's too dangerous further out. They come in for the food. We don't really like the idea, but it's the only way to tag and track. We need to determine habitat domain, and travel radius. Their official name is pink river dolphins.

I'm not going back to Nextdoor. That's over. This research is too important. I'll call them. They'll understand. I'll call Sasha.

The team is huge – 25 exchange students from all over the world and some from Brazil, as well. My tag buddy is Oliviera Fernanda ... something, something, something. These Portugese names are really long. I just call her Dol. It's short for dolphin – she can really swim, and she's the tallest one here. She thinks the name's funny. She laughs at all my stuff. It's so hot here we all have a swim in the cove every afternoon, even the researchers. We have water polo. The Brazilian girls are great swimmers. They'll be the ones to watch at the next Games.

We do a weekly observational report for the project, and her English is really good – her parents are academics in Sao Paulo. We're going down for Carnevale – it's really big in all the towns, not just Rio. She says it's a bit quiet after Carnevale as the parents are quite religious. We're flying down, but we're just tag buddies – it's not some big romance.'

How has the experience added to Ben's Core Skills for Work?

_____

_____

How would you describe his 'Unique Value Proposition' when applying for a research position later?

_____

_____

And Grit – just got a graduate position with ASIO!

Some candidates with, say, an expensive MBA or PhD, may think they should be recompensed immediately. If you're in this situation, the employer will need to be convinced by evidence that this great bit of paper has given you some competitive edge to improve the business bottom line, not that you can wear a red mediaeval gown and funny hat to the Christmas party. If the knowledge gained can improve product or process, then it's worth paying extra, but you must demonstrate this added value with evidence.

You could even link your salary negotiation to the 30/60/90 day plan you used in your interview to show how you will improve employer output, process, and value. A savvy employer will take you at your word, but offer to build the heightened compensation into your performance reviews at those three time points. This is good for you, because it establishes the causal link between your productivity and your benefits – your value.

Know your market

Base your negotiation on your knowledge of the remuneration package range standard in your sector, with an increase reflecting your Unique Value Proposition. They acknowledged it when offering you the position, so now is the time to follow through. The average salary is paid to the average employee, and you're better than that. Go for the top of the range, but negotiate within the range, so they know you're not unrealistic.

Online databases like www.payscale.com will give you the basic information. You can also check out similar roles on recruiter websites like www.hudson.com.au and the big job boards like www.seek.com .

Use the platform to inform

You can use the Seek platform itself to see what the employer's really thinking. If you found your ideal job in the $60-70 000 range, search for the same job in the higher ranges. If you find it there, then that's the top range the employer will consider. Now search again in the lower range. If you find it there, that's the lower figure for the employer. Keep doing this until you can't find the job. This will show you exactly what the employer is thinking on salary and benefits. You can then negotiate confidently at the top of the employer range.

Keep the options operating

Never box yourself into a corner, but keep things fluid until you shake hands on the deal. Don't try blackmail like: 'If you can't give me X, then I'll have to look elsewhere'. There's no need to come across as a tough negotiator who uses confrontation. Statements like: 'I feel I can demonstrate the extra value to justify the package by improving your ..., like I did with my previous employer' will be better received.

Focus on flexibility

There may be some 'hidden value' in the mix at little cost to the employer, but that could have a dollar value for you. You could negotiate a 'work from home' deal that saves you fifteen hours of stress and petrol every week. Not-for-profit organisations may offer salary sacrifice deals that keep the same dollars on the contract, but giving you a tax advantage that's better than a raise!

It's certainly worth negotiating an enhanced deal at the beginning, because if there's a general percentage increase across the organisation, you'll get a stressless double benefit in the future.

There's an old saying: you get what you negotiate, not what you deserve. I'm sure you deserve it all!

Negotiating an enhanced package towards the top of the range shows that you're a realistic person providing value for the employer, and value for yourself.

CONCLUSION

This book has taken you on the journey from career intuition to career outcome. While you can't control your results, you can certainly control your input – your employability. In Australia, your employability skills are now called the Core Skills for Work, and the exercises in this book have given you an unfair advantage in the job market.

You've turned intuition into data

The solid input base has been the Core Skills for Work that you've defined for yourself with *The Australian Career Passport* exercise in Chapter 7. Whatever your position – white collar, blue collar, orange collar, or school collar, understanding and demonstrating your core skills improves your employability.

You've turned data into information, and taken action

You've designed your resume, and your one-page pitch to be consistent with your core skills and relevant to any job you apply for, and to suit the new recruiting environment. Your interview approach has had a makeover, too, helping you to 'read the game' better. This ensures you present relevant information to employers in the language they understand.

You've turned action into outcome

Your job interview and negotiating your benefits package are the short-term outcomes of your work here. The long-term outcome is your improved employability.

XL action

If you've done all the exercises, and you're still uncertain about your future, you may want further career input. This book is about career implementation, but you may need to start with career direction, and my first career book, *The Australian Career Mentor: career guidance for experienced professionals and new graduates*, will help you with that. There's a little overlap between the two books, but they cover different aspects of career development, so you can take the action you need to at the appropriate stage of your career.

I also recommend contacting a qualified career counsellor to take your next career step. As long as the person has a genuine qualification there's no real difference between 'coach' and 'counsellor'. I generally use 'coach' because I think 'counsellor' sounds too clinical. Career coaching isn't molten magic, but a process that brings order out of chaos – to improve your KSAOs. It involves career assessment (including a core skills audit), direction towards labour market information, and then bringing it all together through an interpersonal process with the client. As a career coach, I don't think what I do is particularly brilliant – but what my clients do ... is! I'm sure you'll be brilliant too.

If you undertake one of my career programs, you'll recognise all the skilltasks you've done in this book, because they're based on the suite of exercises my clients have been doing for years. It worked for them, and I hope it's working for you.

We started this book with your intuition, and the work you've done throughout has developed your understanding of your career big picture. Your new 'informed intuition' and ongoing rational anaylsis of your career issues, using the tools in this book, will improve your career action and your career outcome for the present, and the future.

Keep in touch

There is an open invitation to all readers who have bought the book, borrowed it from friends or a library, or are clicking through it on some device, to call me for a chat about any topic covered in the book. Go to www. careermelbourne.com for contact details. This is a genuine offer, because

I want to know how you're using the book for your career development. This is not only personal generosity. We all want outcomes, and your call is my outcome.

The outcome professionals

Career keywords: the Golden Triangle & the Bermuda Triangle; career assessments; *Passport* strategies; fitting the *Passport* into a career program

This book is aimed at individuals implementing career change, but career coaches, careers teachers, and HR professionals also have a stake.

The career professional may have directed their clients to the concepts and exercises in this book. It may also be on the shelves of school, TAFE and university libraries, or be a resource in Careers Centres used by careers staff for student seminars and individual career counselling. It fits into several niches in the career counselling process.

The Golden Triangle of career counselling

The traditional elements of career counselling are:

- administering some form of career assessment;
- linking to occupational information and the educational pathways to jobs; and
- bringing it all together through developing the therapeutic alliance with the client via the chosen communication channels – face-to-face, email, Skype.

Career assessment

Whatever your coaching process, you probably use some form of career assessment to ensure your client doesn't drift out of the Golden Triangle into the Bermuda Triangle. Depending on your setting, and your qualifications and interests, these will be standard assessments, some process you've gotten from the internet, rescued from some filing cabinet, or something you've developed yourself. We all do this, but should recognise that each of these sources of career input has differing levels of reliability and validity – the stronger the reliability and validity, the more confidence in the result.

You will align your career assessment to the nature of your client group. Holland's Self-Directed Search is a common choice – quick, easy, and cheap! While perfectly suitable in a school setting, there are better choices, like the Myers-Briggs Type Indicator and the Strong Interest Inventory for adults. These are unsuitable for a younger audience, though various versions of these two assessments do appear in schools. It's a professional call for you to decide what is appropriate in your setting.

One skills audit resource you should consider is *The Australian Career Passport*. It's based on the *Core Skills for Work Framework* and serves the age range seventeen to seventy!

Pathways – educational and occupational

Your school or institute will have many of the needed resources on occupations, and the work experience program will be beneficial. The Australian Qualifications Framework is an essential resource needing considerable explanation for students on its implications for study choice, and the associated debt.

The therapeutic alliance

Career professionals add value at each apex of the triangle, but the interpersonal relationship developed with the client is the crucial interface. If this goes well, the rest goes well. It's generally accepted that when a counselling interaction is successful, about 4% is due to the placebo effect, 8% to the specific theoretical approach of the counsellor, 8% to the therapeutic alliance between both parties, and 80% to the engagement, energy and motivation of the client.

The area where career professionals could boost professional effectiveness is the therapeutic alliance. A skills audit based on an Australian, rather than US, work culture should help to improve client discussion and interaction – *The Australian Career Passport*.

It's not the intention here to develop a career coaching manual, but to show where the *Passport* fits into the career coaching process, and suggest some strategies to use it effectively.

Passport strategies

The *Passport* identifies core skills. It can be used flexibly by the individual or career professional depending on the purpose for collecting the career data. It's not meant to constrain your approach, but inform it, and improve interaction with your clients.

This book has a readability level suitable for all users, including the young user. On the Flesch-Kincaid, the main body of the text ranks as suitable for Year 12 students. The ᵠ text boxes are at grade 5 level. If your students are totally mortified by this, explain that all US television shows are pitched at the cognitive level of a twelve-year-old.

While *The Australian Career Passport* ᵠ descriptors are targeted at students, they may choose any of the other descriptors they think apply to them. The *Passport* has blank sections enabling students, or you, to add value with extra descriptors suitable for individual circumstances.

Your client can turn the *Passport* into a 360° skills assessment by having other people mark the descriptors. Joining up the intersection points gives a visual of the areas of agreement and discord. The career professional could raise this option in discussion. The joined asterisks aren't a calibrated graph, but a visual pattern of a qualitative estimate.

If your client is a student (of any age) there's some research you may find useful. In 2013, Edith Cowan University reported on an employability skills study of over 1000 business undergraduates. This was before the publication of the *Australian Core Skills Audit* but the findings are still relevant. It discovered considerable discrepancy between student rating of their skills and that of academics rating them. It supports the anecdotal evaluation of many employers:

> *Across the entire sample, 70% of students overrated in comparison to academics and the remaining 30% underrated ... There is substantial evidence supporting the notion that less able students are more likely to overrate their ability and extremely able students ... will underrate.*

Strategies to reduce this discrepancy may be successful with long-term contact with the cohort. Career coaches with limited client contact should at least promote the 360 degree approach to provide external input for discussion, and a reality check.

You may use the *Passport* simply as a discussion starter with the client, and to improve the job application approach. At a more formal level, you could enter the *Passport* information into the *Career Change Generator* using the process described in *The Australian Career Mentor: career guidance for experienced professionals and new graduates*. This is a qualitative data matrix used to tabulate the wide range of client information gathered in career coaching consultations. Once you have the information, you can use it confidently in the career coaching process. There are various entry points for this, depending on your professional context, and consultation aims.

The *Passport* can be integrated easily into existing career programs where a skills audit is needed.

Passport validity

Few skills audits undergo the rigorous validation procedures of the standard career assessments. Most are a compendium of technical skills, 'other' skills, values, attitudes, and the gormless 'attributes'. The *Passport* covers only the core skills – both its strength, and its weakness.

Validity, or the accuracy of the descriptors, was tested with CDAA career counsellors at the 2016 national conference in Melbourne. In the conference workshop, groups wrote skills descriptors based on their professional experience with their different client cohorts. These were later compared with the existing descriptors. There was considerable conceptual overlap, giving confidence in the existing assessment. New descriptors generated by group members have been added to the *Passport* in the appropriate sections. Workshop participants who provided their names for acknowledgement were:

Ann Aulon Airlie Bell Fiona Cotton Lynn Deering Nancy Field Melania Guzman Chris Ling Julie Preste Viv Ride Antoinette Simpson Cathy Sanderson Louise Walsh Zoe Wundenberg

I'd like to thank all 90 workshop participants for their capacity to 'connect and work with others' and for exemplifying 'create and innovate'.

Ethical use of *The Australian Career Passport*:

The data may be aggregated at an organisational, systemic, and national level. The *Passport* enables individuals to improve self-understanding, and it is not intended that it be used to compare individuals competitively in the course selection or job application process. The resource should help people, not disadvantage them.

Positioning the *Passport*

This *Passport* can fit into a number of career development frameworks. An effective career planning framework developed by Naishadh Gadani, a Melbourne career coach, could be seen as involving: self-awareness → opportunity awareness → employability gap → making a choice → self-marketing → self-selling.

The framework starts with self-awareness. You could also see a big arrow going back from self-selling to self-awareness, thus continuing a cycle of the reflection and improvement needed for career development.

Career planning framework	Passport entry points
Self-awareness	The *Passport* promotes self-analysis and self-awareness.
Opportunity awareness	The *Passport* contributes to understanding the perspective of the employer as detailed in the job description or job ad. It also helps job applicants filter out unsuitable jobs to concentrate on high ROI opportunities. The job applicant becomes a high-precision search engine for job opportunities.
Employability gap	The *Passport* defines the individual's core skills. It's the microscope finding the employability gaps that the job applicant must address to improve job targeting.
Making a choice	The *Passport* provides data to inform individual choice. The results can be used with the **Career Change Generator*** for a clear decision on job search action.
Self-marketing	The *Passport* delivers comprehensive information backed by evidence to support the Unique Value Proposition to be conveyed through the resume, and job application.
Self-selling	The knowledge gained by reflecting on the *Passport* categories can be used in the job interview to communicate well with the interviewer to influence the job offer decision.

*The **Career Change Generator** is a qualitative data matrix developed to speed a career decision by considering all relevant information including accredited assessment results. It was presented for the first time in Chapter 6 of **The Australian Career Mentor: career guidance for experienced professionals and new graduates**, pages 81 – 87.

Career coaches will have other career development systems – well-known, or self-generated. It would be good to know how other members of the profession are linking the *Passport* to their preferred systems and resources, and I invite contact on this issue.

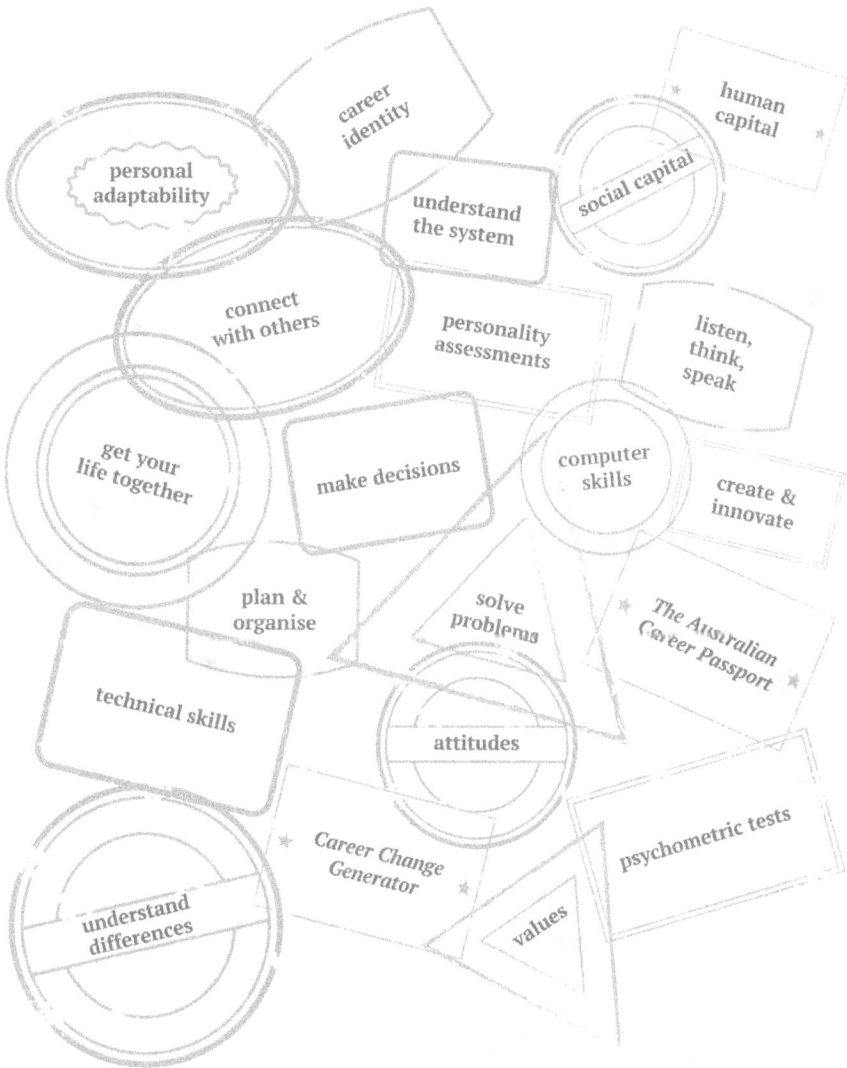

Linking The Australian Career Passport *to existing career programs provides the core skills visa stamp of approval to help your clients cross the career border, and jump the job queue to become a valued citizen in the New World of Work.*

APPENDIX B

Australian Government
Department of Employment

Recruitment methods used by employers

Employers use a wide range of recruitment methods to fill vacancies. Accordingly, it is important that job seekers adopt a variety of job search strategies to avoid missing out on potential employment opportunities. To assist job seekers in this regard, the most common recruitment methods used by employers across Australia are outlined below.[1]

More than half of all vacancies are advertised on the internet or in a newspaper

More than 150,000 vacancies are advertised on internet sites or in newspapers across the country each month. These vacancies are readily accessible and reach a broad audience, however, they often attract high numbers of applicants.

Roughly half of all vacancies are advertised on the internet. In addition to recruitment sites, many vacancies are advertised on employers' websites (this is particularly common for large organisations, including food and retail chains). Some 18 per cent of vacancies are advertised in newspapers, although this figure has declined in recent years and around half of these positions are also advertised on the internet.

Social media
The use of social media to advertise vacancies has been increasing over recent years, although it still remains low. The use of social media is more common in capital cities where around 5 per cent of vacancies are advertised on websites such as Facebook.

Employment agencies are used for about 15 per cent of vacancies

About 15 per cent of vacancies are filled through an employment agency, such as a private recruitment agency, labour hire firm, or Australian Government funded employment services provider[2]. Employment services providers also offer job search advice and training to help job seekers find work.

About one third of vacancies are not formally advertised

Many employers use informal methods to fill their vacancies, including word of mouth, being approached directly by job seekers, or placing a sign in their shop window. Informal methods of recruitment are most commonly used by employers in regional areas, where up to half of vacancies are not formally advertised, or when filling lower skilled vacancies.

Word of mouth
Employers use word of mouth to recruit for 17 per cent[3] of vacancies. Some employers approach potential applicants directly about job opportunities, while others ask existing employees, friends, or family members if they know anyone who may be interested in the position. To avoid missing out on these opportunities it is important that job seekers broaden their social networks and let people know that they are looking for work.

Approached directly by job seekers
Employers consider job seekers who approached them about potential vacancies in their business when filling about 13 per cent[4] of vacancies. Approaching an employer to ask if they have any jobs available or to drop off a résumé can also provide the opportunity for a job seeker to demonstrate their communication skills, initiative and motivation.

---

[1] In the 2014-15 financial year, more than 10,000 employers were interviewed as part of the Department of Employment's *Survey of Employers' Recruitment Experiences*. The insights presented in this paper are based on the results from this survey.
[2] Includes both Job Services Australia providers and Disability Employment Services providers. A new employment services system (jobactive) was introduced on 1 July 2015. Further information on jobactive services is available on the jobactive website.
[3] Figure excludes vacancies that were also advertised on the internet, newspaper or through an employment agency.
[4] Ibid.

This report was produced by the Labour Market Research and Analysis Branch. Further results on the *Survey of Employers' Recruitment Experiences* can be found at www.employment.gov.au/regionalreports or by contacting recruitmentsurveys@employment.gov.au.

References

Arnold, L. 2015. *The Australian Career Mentor: career guidance for experienced professionals and new graduates.* BookPOD

Australian Government Department of Employment, Labour Market Research and Analysis. 2015. *Recruitment methods used by employers.*

Australian Government. 2015. *PS News online,* Edition no.477

Australian Government. 2013. *Core Skills for Work Developmental Framework*

Briggs Myers, I. *et al.*1999. *MBTI Manual: A guide to the development and use of the Myers-Briggs Type Indicator.* Consulting Psychologists Press, and Australian Council for Educational Research

Ellson, S. 2016. *120 ways to achieve your purpose with Linkedin.* 120 Ways publishing

Foundation for Young Australians. 2016. *The New Work Mindset*

Fugate, M. *et al.* 2004. 'Employability: A psycho-social construct, its dimensions, and applications'. *Journal of Vocational Behaviour,* 65, 14-38

Good Education Group. 2016. *The good careers guide.* www.goodcareersguide.com.au

Good Education Group. 2016. *The good universities guide 2016*

Government of Western Australia. 2014. *Workplace Learning Skills Journal.* School Curriculum and Standards Authority

Jackson, D. 2013. *Self-assessment of employability skill outcomes among undergraduates and alignment with academic ratings.* ECU Publications

Kramer, E.P. 2012. *Active Interviewing.* Cengage Learning

Stein, L.I. 1974. 'The Doctor-Nurse Game' in *Rehabilitation nursing: perspectives and applications.* Mc Graw-Hill

But there's more ...

If you've found this book useful – if you've seen yourself in the scenarios, thought about the issues, and pushed yourself with the exercises then you're in a better place for career implementation. You may want some extra help by taking some of the following career packs.

The *Career Voucher* is a two-session individual career direction program expanding on the ideas in this book, and includes a thorough CV review and accredited career assessment.

If you've found a career direction and want to progress it, then the *Matrix Method* career implementation program will be helpful. This is a three-hour individual job search program looking at how to engage with the employer and recruiter to get you on their screen.

The *Six Week Career Change* program is good if you already have some idea of where you're going and want to test it out. It combines the career direction stage with the job search stage so you can decide on your career direction, and immediately test it out in the marketplace with targeted job applications. The program includes several coffee catch-up personal meetings with me to keep you on track and explore expanding options. This program gives you the hard information over the first three weeks, and the second phase coaches you in how to use it creatively and effectively. There's coffee and a biscuit as well!

Once you have the interview invitation, the *Interview Skills Program* will help you further understand the employer perspective to present yourself well. This is a three-hour individual program with 30 days help-desk support to guide you as you approach your interviews.

I offer all these packs in person, in the Melbourne CBD, but can also offer them remotely.

You can see what you get with these programs at www.careermelbourne. com and then email or call me for further information or to make a booking. I don't respond to texts. I've got an older phone and the touch pad is too small. I also don't want to spend my life sending texts all over the world to people I've never met. I became a career coach to talk with people – not contract Text Thumb Syndrome! Please feel free to call or email me for more information on any of the career packs, or for a no obligations chat about your career direction.

The author

Lawrence Arnold, FRSA, MBTI, MA, Grad. Cert. Career Counselling, has combined intuition and education with a bit of risk-taking to achieve his career goals. After some years as an organisational consultant, he had a Jungian moment when he decided to become a career counsellor. He combines private practice in the Melbourne CBD with providing outplacement services to national and international companies.

Writing has always been part of the mix, whether popular career articles in the *Herald Sun* or articles targeting CDAA career professionals in the *Australian Career Practitioner* and the Australian Careers Service publications. His first book, *The Australian Career Mentor: career guidance for experienced professionals and new graduates*, introduced the *Australian Core Skills Audit* and focused on career direction. This second book targets career implementation, and introduces *The Australian Career Passport* to people 17 – 70 across all occupations.

Public seminars and conference presentations add a bit of spice to the mix. He has been a strong supporter of the Career Development Association of Australia presence at Melbourne career expos over many years, presenting *The Ten Commandments of Employability* seminar to audiences of 100+. He has contributed to the professional development of other career coaches by presenting the conference paper, *STEM and BRANCH: assessing and rating employability skills individually and across the Australian economy using the Australian Core Skills Audit* at the CDAA 2016 national conference in Melbourne.

He is a Life Fellow of the Royal Society of Arts, being elected for his contribution to professional writing in the career sector. The Royal Society of Arts was established in Britain in 1754 with the mission of improving the national social and intellectual infrastructure with thought-leading projects that make a difference for people. Benjamin Franklin, Charles Dickens, and Albert Einstein were members. Lawrence is proud to round out his professional life contributing to this 250-year-old society from the past, by writing for the future.